D1761591

# Modula-2 Wizard
## A Programmer's Reference

## Richard S. Wiener

*Department of Computer Science*
*University of Colorado at Colorado Springs*

John Wiley & Sons, Inc.
New York • Chichester • Brisbane • Toronto • Singapore

**Publisher:** Stephen Kippur
**Editor:** Theron Shreve
**Managing Editor:** Katherine Bolster
**Electronic Production Services:** The Publisher's Network

Wiley books can be used as premiums to promote
products or services, for training, or in mail-order catalogs.
For information on quantity discounts, please write to the
Special Sales Department, John Wiley & Sons, Inc.

**Library of Congress Cataloging-in-Publication Data**

Wiener, Richard, 1941-
  Modula-2 wizard's.

  Includes index.
  1. Modula-2 (Computer program language)
  I. Title.   II. Title: Modula-two wizard's.
QA76.73.M63W54   1986   005.13'3   86-11077
ISBN 0-471-84853-0

Printed in the United States of America

86 87 10 9 8 7 6 5 4 3 2 1

*This book is dedicated to my closest friend,*
*my wife Sheila.*

# RELATED TITLES OF INTEREST
# FROM JOHN WILEY & SONS, INC:

| | |
|---|---|
| Ashley/Fernandez | COBOL: A PROFESSIONAL PROGRAMMER'S REFERENCE* <br> PC DOS 2nd Edition |
| Devlin/Skvarcius | LISP: A PROGRAMMER'S REFERENCE* |
| Foster | PROLOG: A PROGRAMMER'S REFERENCE* |
| Morse/Albert | 8087 PRIMER <br> THE 80286 ARCHITECTURE |
| Skvarcius | ADA: A PROGRAMMER'S REFERENCE |
| Tabler | IBM PC ASSEMBLY LANGUAGE |
| Wiener | PASCAL WIZARD PROGRAMMER'S REFERENCE* <br> JOURNAL OF PASCAL, ADA & MODULA-2 |

An * indicates a forthcoming title.

# Contents

## Preface

Modula-2 is a new and powerful software development language. Introduced by Niklaus Wirth in 1980, it extends Pascal in two directions.

Modula-2 provides support for the development of large software systems using object-oriented programming and modern software engineering. Modula-2 also provides low-level features similar to those in the C programming language.

This book is aimed at programmers and software development professionals with some programming experience in Pascal or Modula-2. It is intended to be a comprehensive reference guide that presents all facets of the Modula-2 language in an easily accessible manner.

The book contains many fully tested program segments that illustrate all of the features of the Modula-2 language. The source code for a powerful screen input/output utility package is presented in its entirety. This package illustrates many important low-level programming techniques applicable in an MS-DOS Modula-2 environment.

Existing input/output libraries as well as the latest proposed international standard Modula-2 libraries are described in the book. These form the basis for the software development environment surrounding Modula-2 programming.

The latest changes to the Modula-2 language are presented and summarized. A detailed description of some important, new, non-standard features that will be implemented by Borland International in Turbo Modula-2 are presented in detail.

**Acknowledgments**

I thank the fine software engineering team at Logitech, Inc., Redwood City, CA for producing an outstanding professional Modula-2 software development environment under MS-DOS. I thank Chris Cale at Logitech for his help in providing continual updates and improvements to the Modula-2 software development system.

I thank Mike Weisert at Borland International for providing important information relating to Turbo Modula-2.

I thank Theron Shreve, editor at John Wiley and Sons, for his confidence in me and assistance in this project.

I thank Dr. Lewis Pinson, a good friend and colleague at the University of Colorado at Colorado Springs for his help in reviewing this manuscript.

I thank Erik Wiener, my son, for his tremendous help in reviewing and preparing the manuscript.

Although they are not directly related to this book, I am grateful to Steve Moskowitz, Paul Trautman, Stuart Greenfield and my brother Paul Wiener for several decades of very close friendship.

Finally I wish to express my love and appreciation to Sheila, my wife, for her confidence and love during this project. It is to her that I dedicate this book.

Richard S. Wiener
*Department of Computer Science*
*University of Colorado at Colorado Springs*

## How to Use This Book

The book contains five sections and several appendixes.

Section 1 presents an overview of the Modula-2 language. There are over 100 figures that contain tables and Modula-2 program segments to illustrate every aspect of the Modula-2 language. The program segments should be studied carefully. They illustrate the use of every language construct.

Whenever appropriate, there are discussions entitled *Style, Hazard, and Software Engineering* interspersed throughout Section 1.

The discussions entitled *Style* present tips relating to the layout and format of Modula-2 programs. Programs are for people as well as for machines. The readability of a program greatly affects its cost of maintenance. Great care has been taken in establishing a good role model for program style.

The discussions entitled *Hazard* present common programming errors and their correction.

The discussions entitled *Software Engineering* discuss the use of a construct from a software engineering perspective.

Section 2 may be of particular interest to Pascal programmers who wish to compare that language with Modula-2. The differences between the two languages are summarized in this section.

Sections 3 and 4 are references that contain existing and proposed libraries. These libraries form the environment that surrounds all Modula-2 programming projects.

Section 5 presents the recent changes in Modula-2. It also presents some new, exciting, and non-standard features that will be contained in the Borland International Turbo Modula-2.

The four appendixes and reference card are presented as a quick reference guide.

# SECTION 1

# Modula-2 Language Overview

- **Brief History of Modula-2**
- **Programming Style**
- **Lexical Structure**
- **Declarations**
- **Data Types**
- **Scalar Types**
- **Structured Types**
- **Pointer Variables**
- **Expressions**
- **Type Conversion and Type Transfer**
- **Predefined Functions and Procedures**
- **Sequence Control Structures**
- **Branching Structures**
- **Iterative Structures**
- **Procedures and Procedure Functions**
- **Recursion**
- **Internal Modules**
- **Library Modules**
- **Data Abstraction and Opaque Types**
- **Low-level Features**
- **Processes**

## Brief History of Modula-2

Modula-2 is a descendant of Pascal and Modula. In 1975, less than 10 years after designing Pascal, Niklaus Wirth developed the experimental language Modula to investigate the programming problems associated with multiprocessing systems. Wirth discontinued his Modula language work after spending a year at Xerox Palo Alto Research Center. There he gained experience with the Alto work station computer and the Mesa programming language. In 1977, Dr. Wirth embarked on a research project at the Institute fur Informatik of ETH, Zurich, whose goal was to design a computer system coupled to a new computer language to support modern software engineering. The research led to the development of the Lilith™ computer and the Modula-2 language. Modula-2 was demonstrated on a PDP-11™ computer in 1979. The language's definition was published as a technical report in March 1980. The first compiler was released in 1981.

Modula-2 was developed during the same period as Ada and addresses the same need—a language for developing large and reliable software systems. Modula-2 retains the simplicity and readability of Pascal, contains the low-level power of C and the high-level data and functional abstraction features of Ada.

## Programming Style

The physical layout of a program, its style, affects its readability and its maintainability. Programs are not just grist serving as the input to a compiler but are read and analyzed by people. Indeed, a well-formatted program with suitable supporting comments is often a "deliverable" that provides important documentation in support of the problem-solving process.

Modula-2, like most modern programming languages, is expressed as a free-format character string. The programmer has virtually infinite latitude in deciding how to control both horizontal and vertical white space. Although no particular style is optimum, consistency is important. Suggestions about style will be inserted in context as new constructs are introduced. It is the responsibility of the programmer to experiment with various style options and to develop a consistent style.

It is the view of this author that a good programming style should balance efficiency of expression with clarity. This may mean the addition of extra lines of code in the interest of creating "clean," easy-to-read code. Figure 1.1 shows four of the many possible alternative representations of the IF THEN

ELSE construct. The last alternative is the one that has been adopted by this author and the one that will be used in programs and program segments.

```
                                (a)
IF ( a >= 15 ) AND ( b < c * d ) THEN e := f; ELSE e := g;
END;
```

```
                                (b)
IF ( a >= 15 ) AND ( b < c * d ) THEN
  e := f; ELSE
  e := g;
END;
```

```
                                (c)
IF ( a >= 15 ) AND ( b < c * d )
THEN e := f;
ELSE e := g;
END;
```

```
                                (d)
IF ( a >= 15 ) AND ( b < c * d )
THEN
  e := f;
ELSE
  e := g;
END(* if then *);
```

**Figure 1.1** Alternative programming styles

# Lexical Structures

The lexical elements of Modula-2 include identifiers, literal constants, operators, delimiters, comments, and separators.

## Identifiers

An identifier must start with a letter and may then be followed with a sequence of either letters or digits. Underscores and spaces cannot be used as part of an identifier. An identifier may be arbitrarily long and all characters are significant. Some vendors of Modula-2 systems may impose implementation restrictions on the number of significant characters.

letters:

abcdefghijklmnopqrstuvwxyz

ABCDEFGHIJKLMNOPQRSTUVWXYZ

digits:

0123456789

A Modula-2 compiler distinguishes lower-case letters from upper-case letters. Thus the identifier MyName is distinct from myname, which is distinct from MYNAME.

All reserved words of Modula-2 are strictly upper-case.

Identifiers are used to name variables, types, constants, procedures, and modules. Examples of illegal identifiers are given in Figure 1.2.

```
2name      my_name     your-name      $name      name$      %raise
```

**Figure 1.2** Illegal identifiers

Examples of illegal identifiers are given in Figure 1.3.

```
i      j      k      nePtune      Neptune      NepTune      name1
name2      m1      m1234j
```

**Figure 1.3** Legal identifiers

## *Style:*

A convention used in this book is that all programmer-defined identifiers are strictly lower case. This unburdens one's memory from having to recall the spelling of an identifier (e.g., is the procedure name VectorSum, Vectorsum, VECTORSUM, or vectorsum?).

Unfortunately, many of the standard library modules use mixed-case identifiers such as WriteString, WriteLn, and ReadReal. The argument in support of using mixed-case identifiers is that they promote readability. In the view of this author, this advantage is more than offset by the extra burden in typing and remembering the spelling of identifiers.

## *Hazard:*

Many if not most compilation errors experienced by beginning Modula-2 programmers relate to case sensitivity. A typical example is given in Figure 1.4.

```
       Incorrect                          Correct

          (a)
    for i := 1 to 5 do
      . . .

          (b)                               (d)
    FOR i := 1 to 5 DO              FOR i := 1 TO 5 DO
      . . .                           . . .

          (c)                               (e)
    WHILE ( a >= 1 ) do            WHILE ( a >= 1 ) DO
      . . .
```

**Figure 1.4** Typical case-sensitivity error

## Integer Literals

An integer literal is formed by a sequence of digits with an optional radix indicator following the last character. If the radix indicator is B, the number is interpreted as an octal (base 8) integer. If the radix indicator is H, the number is interpreted as a hexadecimal (base 16) integer. A hexadecimal literal must begin with the digit 0 and may be followed with other digits or the letters A, B, C, D, E, or F. The absence of a radix indicator is interpreted as a decimal integer. Some legal integer literals are shown in Figure 1.5.

```
   62    0ABCDEFH    24B    000A234FH    0CBA1H
```

**Figure 1.5** Some legal integer literals

Figure 1.6 shows some illegal integer literals.

```
75.1      - Decimal point not legal
ABCDEFH   - Hexidecimal literal must begin with digit 0
0ABCDEF   - Hexidecimal literal must end with radix indicator
59B       - Digit 9 is not in the octal range
1,222     - Comma not legal
0BEFGH    - Character G not in the hexidecimal range
```

**Figure 1.6** Some illegal integer literals

## Real Literals

Real literals contain a sequence of digits representing the whole number part, followed by a decimal point, followed by an optional sequence of digits representing the fraction part, and an optional scale factor. The scale factor, if present, is composed of the character E optionally followed by a sign ( + or − ) and a sequence of digits representing a power of 10.

Figure 1.7 displays some legal real literals.

```
0.0   0.   1.23435   1.234E-2   1.E03   1.0E-6
```

**Figure 1.7**  Some legal real literals

Figure 1.8 displays some illegal real literals.

```
.7          - Reals must begin with a digit
27.3E24.2 - Scale factor cannot contain a decimal point
42.3e22   - Upper case 'E' required
```

**Figure 1.8**  Some illegal real literals

## Boolean Literals

The two Boolean literal constants are given in Figure 1.9. Note that they are spelled with upper-case characters without quotation marks or apostrophes around them.

```
TRUE        FALSE
```

**Figure 1.9**  Boolean literals

### *Hazard:*

Using quotation marks or apostrophes in assigning a Boolean variable a Boolean literal as in:

```
b:= "TRUE"
```

or

```
b:= 'FALSE'
```

## Character Literals

Character literals are enclosed either in apostrophes or quotation marks. The literals 'z' and "z" are equivalent.

Control characters that do not have a graphical representation may be represented by their ordinal values expressed as integer octals followed by the letter c instead of the usual radix octal indicator B. For example, the control character backspace, ASCII value 8 (10 in octal), is represented by the character literal 10C.

## String Literals

String literals, like character literals, are enclosed either in apostrophes or quotation marks. Thus the string "nice day" is equivalent to 'nice day.'

A string enclosed in apostrophes may not contain an apostrophe, nor may strings enclosed in quotation marks contain a quotation mark.

Figure 1.10 displays some legal characters and strings.

```
'memory management'
"Marc's book"
'Erik said "how are you today." '
"!@#$%^&*()"
' " '
" ' "
' '
```

**Figure 1.10** Some legal characters and strings

Figure 1.11 shows some illegal characters and strings.

```
'Sheila's pen.'              - Contains two apostrophes
"Marc said, "hello again"."  - Contains two quotation marks
49C                          - Digit 9 not an octal digit
300C                         - Value too large for character
                               set
```

**Figure 1.11** Some illegal characters and strings

In Modula-2, like in C, there is no formal string type. A string is a contiguous set of characters residing in an array of base type CHAR with index range 0 to some constant upper limit. If a string literal does not fill the fixed size array that the literal is assigned to, it is terminated with the null character, 0C. This is illustrated in Figure 1.12. Note that the assignment of the literal ABCEDFGHIJ to the string variable s does not cause the compiler to append the null character, 0C, to the end of the array because this string literal fills up the array.

```
VAR s : ARRAY[ 0..9 ] OF CHAR;
s := "MODULA";

array s          -->   M O D U L A 0C

index position -->    0 1 2 3 4 5 6


s := "ABCDEFGHIJ"

array s          -->   A B C D E F G H I J

index position -->    0 1 2 3 4 5 6 7 8 9
```

**Figure 1.12** Strings

## Set Literals

Set data types are allowable in Modula-2. BITSETS are predefined.

Every BITSET literal corresponds to a bitstring (a binary number).

We show some properly formed and improperly formed BITSET literals in Figure 1.13 and show the relationship between BITSET literals and bitstrings. A 16-bit machine is assumed.

```
                (a) Properly formed BITSET literals

Bitset                        Bitstring
------                        ---------
{}                            0000000000000000

{ 0, 1, 2 }                   0000000000000111

{ 1, 4, 9, 12, 15 }           1001001000010010

                (b) Improperly formed BITSET literals

[ 3, 5, 7 ]    - Wrong brackets used

{ 1, 12, 16 } - 16 out of range of 16 bit machine

{ a, b, c }    - a, b, and c are not constants
```

**Figure 1.13** Properly and improperly formed BITSET literals

## Reserved Words

In Figure 1.14, the reserved words in Modula-2 are displayed. It is illegal to use a reserved word as an identifier.

```
AND                              LOOP
ARRAY                            MOD
BEGIN                            MODULE
BY                               NOT
CASE                             OF
CONST                            OR
DEFINITION                       POINTER
DIV                              PROCEDURE
DO                               QUALIFIED
ELSE                             RECORD
ELSIF                            REPEAT
END                              RETURN
EXIT                             SET
EXPORT                           THEN
FOR                              TO
FROM                             TYPE
IF                               UNTIL
IMPLEMENTATION                   VAR
IMPORT                           WHILE
IN                               WITH
```

**Figure 1.14** Reserved words in Modula-2

## Comments

A comment in Modula-2, as in other languages, is program text that is ignored by a compiler. Comments are used to add clarity to a source listing and are only for a human reader. Some implementations of Modula-2 may use special types of comments as compiler directives. For example, (*$L + *) may direct the compiler to produce a detailed compiler listing.

Comments are delimited by the two-character symbols (* to begin a comment and *) to end a comment.

Comments may be nested. Figure 1.15 illustrates a practical application of nested comments. Here a block of code that already contains comments is blocked out with an additional pair of comments. This is useful in debugging.

There is no limit to the number of nesting levels for comments.

```
(*
IF ( a > b )
THEN
    . . .
END(* if then *);
WHILE ( c < d ) DO
    . . .
END(* while loop *);
*)
```

**Figure 1.15** Practical application of nested comments

## Operators and Delimiters

Operators are lexical elements that denote that a particular action or operation is to be performed. Some operators are denoted by reserved words. Other operators are denoted by several nonalphabetic characters.

Delimiters mark the beginning or end of other entities and are given by either reserved words or by several nonalphabetic characters. Figure 1.16 shows the nonalphabetic operators and delimiters of Modula-2.

```
+          unary plus, addition, set union
-          unary minus, subtraction, set difference
*          multiplication, set intersection
/          real division, symmetric set difference
:=         assignment
&          boolean and
=          equal
<>         not equal
#          not equal
>          greater than
<          less than
>=         greater than or equal, superset
<=         less than or equal, subset
^          pointer dereference
()         parentheses
[]         array index brackets, subrange brackets
{}         set braces
(* *)      comment delimiters
..         subrange delimiter
.          period, qualified identifier
,          used to separate entities
;          used as separator between statements
|          used in case statements
```

**Figure 1.16** Nonalphabetic operators and delimiters

## Separators

A separator in Modula-2 is white space (one or more blanks), a new line, or a comment. None of the lexical elements described earlier except comments may have embedded separators. A blank embedded in a character string is not a separator because it is a syntactically legal part of the entity.

In a program, a separator may appear between any two lexical elements.

## Declarations

Five classes of entities must be declared in Modula-2 programs: modules, procedures, types, variables, and constants. There are no labels allowed in Modula-2, thus no goto statements.

The five classes of entities may be declared in any order (i.e., modules may be declared within procedures, variable declarations may precede type declarations, etc.).

An entity must be declared before it is used. Thus, as a matter of practice, it is necessary to declare a type before declaring variables (objects) to be of the given type.

## Constant Declarations

Constants are data objects whose values never change. In a constant declaration, an identifier is associated with a literal constant. The identifier may be used instead of the literal constant throughout a program.

The syntax of a constant declaration is given as:

```
CONST
   ident1 = literal1;
   ident2 = literal2;
   . . .
```

In Modula-2, constants may be defined in terms of constant expressions (expressions involving other constants that are either literals or previously defined constants).

## *Software Engineering:*

If it is possible, it is desirable to express a constant in terms of one or more previously defined constants so that if such a previously defined constant is changed during program maintenance, there are no fall-out effects.

When the value of a constant must be changed in a large program, only the declaration (definition) of the constant must be changed, just once. On the other hand, if literal constants are used, finding all of their occurences would generally be difficult. A serious programming error could occur if one or more such literal constants were missed.

Constants often provide important insights related to problem-solving decisions that might not otherwise be evident. For example, if a constant citytax is defined as 0.05, the assignment statement,

```
cost := price * (1.0 + citytax)
```

makes more sense than the assignment statement,

```
cost := price * 1.05;
```

Using constants in a program greatly adds to the readability of the program. Figure 1.17 illustrates the enhanced readability of code using constants.

```
CONST
      pi      = 3.14159265;
      twopi   = 2.0 * pi;
      . . .

circumference := twopi * radius;
area := pi * radius * radius;
```

**Figure 1.17**  Constants aid in program readability

Figure 1.18 displays some typical constant declarations.

## *Style:*

The identifier names and definitions are lined up in tabular form in Figure 1.18. This makes such a declaration easier to read.

```
CONST
      sentinel    = '#';
      upperbound = 1499;
      lowerbound = 16;
      debug       = FALSE;
      prompt      = "What is your name --> ";
CONST
      nullset     = {};
      bell        = 7C;
      arraysize   = 100;
      coprocessor = TRUE;
```

**Figure 1.18** Typical constant declarations

## Type Declarations

There are two classes of type declarations in Modula-2: transparent and opaque. A transparent type is fully specified at its point of declaration. An opaque type may only be declared in a definition module (see Definition Modules in this section). Its specification is given in the associated implementation module (see Implementation Modules).

The syntax of a type declaration is given as:

```
TYPE
  ident1 = type1;
  ident2 = type2;
  . . .
```

Figure 1.19 illustrates a typical type declaration.

```
TYPE
      numeral  = [ '0' .. '9' ];

      digit    = [ 0..9 ];

      data     = ARRAY[ 1..1000 ] OF REAL;

      ptr      = POINTER TO node;

      list     = RECORD
                    value : INTEGER;
                    next  : list;
                 END(* record *);

      tree     = POINTER TO treenode;

      treenode = RECORD
                    info  : CARDINAL;
                    left  : tree;
                    right : tree;
                 END(* record *);
```

**Figure 1.19** A typical type declaration

Figure 1.20 illustrates an opaque type.

```
DEFINITION MODULE opaqueillustration;
   ...

   TYPE opaquetype;
   (* Specification given in implementation module. *)
   ...
END opaqueillustration.
```

**Figure 1.20**  An opaque type

## *Style:*

Type declaration blocks should be lined up in tabular form as illustrated in Figure 1.19.

## Variable Declarations

The syntax of variable declarations is given as:

```
VAR
    ident1,
    ident2 : type 1;
    ident 3 : type 2;
    . . .
```

The type required in a variable declaration may be either a single identifier or an anonymous type definition expression. Typical variable declaration blocks are illustrated in Figure 1.21. Variable realdata is declared in terms of an anonymous type (see Assignment Compatibility).

```
VAR
    realnumber : REAL;
    intnumber  : INTEGER;
    cardnumber : CARDINAL;
    realdata   : ARRAY[ 1..100 ] OF REAL;
    var1, var2 : CHAR;

TYPE
    name = ARRAY[ 0..19 ] OF CHAR;

VAR
    namedata : ARRAY[ 1..size ] OF name;
```

**Figure 1.21**  Typical variable declaration blocks

## Data Types

A data type may be defined as sets of Values and Operations, where Values represents a set of values and Operations represents a set of operations.

Every constant, variable, and expression is associated with a particular data type. All constants and variables must be declared before their use. Constants are "typecast" according to the literal that is used in their definition. For example, the constant declaration, speed = 36.5, casts the constant speed as type real, speed = 14 casts the constant speed as type cardinal, and speed = −5 casts the constant speed as type integer.

Data types are either scalar or structured. Scalar data types are indivisible entities whereas structured data types are made up of collections of still smaller entities.

### *Software Engineering:*

Modula-2 is a strongly typed language. This implies that the compiler enforces a set of rules governing the use of data types. For each type declared, the compiler ensures that the value assigned to a variable of the given type belongs to the set Values and that the operations performed on the variable belong to the set Operations. This checking establishes consistency of usage for a given data type and prevents the misuse of a given data type.

## Scalar Data Types

### Integer and Cardinal

The integer and cardinal data types in Modula-2 are denoted INTEGER and CARDINAL, respectively. Cardinals are non-negative integers. A typical variable declaration is:

```
VAR
  a, b : INTEGER;
  c, d : CARDINAL:
```

## Software Engineering:

A cardinal declaration should be used whenever an integer-type variable is to be restricted to nonnegative values. This is determined from the context of a problem. Frequently, index variables in loops may be declared as cardinal. The advantage of such cardinal variable declarations is that the compiler and runtime system can enforce the logical constraint that the cardinal variable can only assume nonnegative values.

The set of allowable values for integers and cardinals are implementation dependent.

On a 16-bit machine, the typical range of values for integers is: $-32768$ . . . $32767$. The typical range for cardinals is 0 . . .65535.

On a 32-bit machine, the typical range of values for integers is: $-2147483648$ . . . $2147483647$. The typical range for cardinals is 0 . . . 4294967295.

The set of allowable operations for both integer and cardinal types includes addition, subtraction, multiplication, division, modulus, and negation. Figure 1.22 lists the symbols for integer and cardinal operations.

```
Operation                    Symbol
---------                    ------
addition                       +
subtraction                    -
multiplication                 *
division                      DIV
modulus                       MOD
negation                       -
```

**Figure 1.22** Allowable operations for types integer and cardinal

## Hazard:

A common error is to use the / symbol for division of two integers or two cardinals rather than the DIV operator. The compiler will trap such an error.

Division by zero leads to an integer or cardinal overflow error that is implementation dependent. Most systems cause program execution to halt with the "divide by zero error" message.

The results of division are truncated. For example,

$13 \text{ DIV } 3 = 4$

$-7 \text{ DIV } 2 = -3$

$24 \text{ DIV } 7 = 3$

The MOD operation is defined only for positive operands as follows:

if quotient $=$ a DIV b and remainder $=$ a MOD b,

then a $=$ quotient $*$ b $+$ remainder,

where $0 < =$ remainder $<$ b.

Some implementations may support short and long integers and/or cardinals (see Section 5, The Borland Turbo Modula-2).

## Real

The real data type in Modula-2 is denoted REAL. A typical variable declaration is:

```
VAR
    x, y : REAL;
```

The set of allowable operations for the real data type includes addition, subtraction, multiplication, division, and negation.

Figure 1.23 lists the symbols for real operations.

```
Operation                Symbol
---------                ------
addition                   +
subtraction                -
multiplication             *
division                   /
negation                   -
```

**Figure 1.23**  Allowable operations for type real

*Hazard:*

Division by zero leads to an overflow error that is implementation dependent. Most systems cause program execution to halt with "divide by zero error" message.

Some implementations may support short and long reals (see Section 5, The Borland Turbo Modula-2).

## Boolean

The Boolean data type in Modula-2 is denoted BOOLEAN. A typical variable declaration is:

```
VAR
    flag1, flag2 : BOOLEAN;
```

The set of allowable values for this type is (FALSE, TRUE). The set of allowable operations includes conjunction, disjunction, and negation.

Figure 1.24 lists the symbols for Boolean operations.

```
Operation              Symbol
---------              ------
conjunction            AND or &
disjunction            OR
negation               NOT
```

**Figure 1.24** Symbols for Boolean operations

Figure 1.25 lists the truth tables that precisely define the meaning of AND, OR, and NOT.

| a | b | a & b | a OR b | NOT a |
|---|---|---|---|---|
| FALSE | FALSE | FALSE | FALSE | TRUE |
| TRUE | FALSE | FALSE | TRUE | FALSE |
| FALSE | TRUE | FALSE | TRUE | TRUE |
| TRUE | TRUE | TRUE | TRUE | FALSE |
| FALSE | UNDEFINED | FALSE | UNDEFINED | TRUE |
| TRUE | UNDEFINED | UNDEFINED | TRUE | FALSE |
| UNDEFINED | TRUE | UNDEFINED | UNDEFINED | UNDEFINED |
| UNDEFINED | FALSE | UNDEFINED | UNDEFINED | UNDEFINED |
| UNDEFINED | UNDEFINED | UNDEFINED | UNDEFINED | UNDEFINED |

**Figure 1.25** Truth Table For Boolean Operators

Short-circuit evaluation is performed, as is evident in Figure 1.25. This implies that the order of evaluation of Boolean expressions is critical (i.e., a AND b is not necessarily the same as b AND a). In a conjunction of one or more operands, the evaluation stops as soon as a value FALSE is detected. In a disjunction of one or more operands, the evaluation stops as soon as a value TRUE is detected.

A Boolean data type may be considered to be an enumeration type (see Enumeration Type) defined as:

```
TYPE BOOLEAN = ( FALSE, TRUE ) ;
```

Any of the functions and procedures defined for enumeration types may also be applied to a Boolean type.

## *Software Engineering:*

In setting up Boolean expressions, the short-circuit evaluation may be exploited to accomplish error protection in a program. For example, for real variables a, b, and c the following expression cannot cause a divide by zero error:

```
IF ( b > 0 ) AND ( c > = a / b )
THEN
   . . .
```

In Pascal, which does not support short-circuit evaluation, the previous expression would have to be written:

```
if ( b > 0 )
then
  if ( c > = c / b )
  then
   . . .
```

As another example, if the array data is declared as

```
VAR data : ARRAY[ 1..1000 ] OF CARDINAL;
```

the following loop structure protects against an index range error:

```
WHILE ( index < = 1000 ) AND ( data[ index ] # 17 ) DO
   . . .
```

## Character

The character type in Modula-2 is denoted CHAR. A typical variable declaration is:

```
VAR
    ch1, ch2 : CHAR;
```

The allowable values for type character are implementation dependent. Most implementations use the American Standard Code for Information Interchange (ASCII) character set. This set includes both printable and control characters. Figure 1.26 displays the ASCII character set with octal codes.

| First Digits | | | | | Last Digits | | | |
|---|---|---|---|---|---|---|---|---|
| | 0 | 1 | 2 | 3 | 4 | 5 | 6 | 7 |
| 00 | nul | soh | stx | etx | eot | enq | ack | bel |
| 01 | bs | tab | lf | vt | f.f | cr | so | si |
| 02 | dle | dc1 | dc2 | dc3 | dc4 | nak | syn | etb |
| 03 | can | em | sub | esc | fs | gs | rs | us |
| 04 | sp | ! | " | # | $ | % | & | ' |
| 05 | ( | ) | * | + | , | – | . | / |
| 06 | 0 | 1 | 2 | 3 | 4 | 5 | 6 | 7 |
| 07 | 8 | 9 | : | ; | < | = | > | ? |
| 10 | @ | A | B | C | D | E | F | G |
| 11 | H | I | J | K | L | M | N | O |
| 12 | P | Q | R | S | T | U | V | W |
| 13 | X | Y | Z | [ | \ | ] | ^ | ‾ |
| 14 | | a | b | c | d | e | f | g |
| 15 | h | i | j | k | l | m | n | o |
| 16 | p | q | r | s | t | u | v | w |
| 17 | x | y | z | { | \| | } | | del |

**Figure 1.26** ASCII Table

There are no special operations defined for the character type except the relational operations that are defined for all scalar types (see Expressions).

### *Hazard:*

A failure to enclose a character literal in either apostrophes or quotation marks is illegal. For example, the following assignment statement is illegal:

```
ch := B;
```

This assignment statement should be given as:

```
ch := 'B';
```

## Enumeration

Enumeration types are defined by the programmer.
The syntax of an enumeration type is given as:

```
TYPE
    ident = (enum1, enum2, . . ., enumk);
```

An example of some enumeration types are given in Figure 1.27.

```
TYPE

    gender = ( male, female );

    order  = ( largest, larger, large, small, smaller,
               smallest );

    days   = ( Mon, Tues, Wed, Thurs, Fri, Sat, Sun );

    months = ( Jan, Feb, Mar, Apr, May, Jun, Jul, Aug, Sep,
               Oct, Nov, Dec );
```

**Figure 1.27** Example of enumeration types

No more than one enumeration type containing a particular identifier can be defined. All of the identifiers for a given enumeration type are constants.

The values of enumeration types are ordered according to the order shown in the declaration. For example, in Figure 1.27, male is smaller than female, and larger is smaller than large.

A mapping exists between the set of values of an enumeration type and the set of cardinals { 0, 1, . . ., n } (see Type Conversion and Type Transfer). The ordinal value of the first enumeration constant is 0, the next is 1, and so forth.

There are no specialized operations defined on enumeration types.

## *Software Engineering:*

Enumeration types usually add clarity to a program. Logical errors may be avoided by the use of enumeration types. For example, suppose the months are defined as a cardinal type as follows:

```
VAR month : CARDINAL;
```

instead of

```
VAR month : months;
```

It is understood that 1 represents January, 2 represents February, and so on. The expression,

```
IF month = 5
THEN
   . . .
```

is equivalent to the expression,

```
IF month = May
THEN
   . . .
```

This seems innocent enough. Suppose another cardinal variable, earnings, has been declared. Then the following expression is legal although meaningless if month is declared as a cardinal type:

```
month : = earnings * 2;
```

If month were declared as an enumeration type, the above expression would be flagged as an error by the compiler.

## Subrange

A subrange type contains values that are a contiguous subset of the value set of another scalar type called the base type. The operations for a subrange type are inherited from the base type.

The syntax of a subrange type is given as:

```
TYPE ident = | lowerlimit . . upperlimit |;
```

A typical variable declaration for a subrange type is the following:

```
VAR
    age        : [ 20..40 ];
    weekend    : [ Sat .. Sun ];
    coldmonths : [ Jan..Mar ];
```

Some additional types are given in Figure 1.28.

```
TYPE
    uppercase   = [ 'A'..'Z' ];
    lowercase   = [ 'a'..'z' ];
    singledigit = [ 0..9 ];
```

**Figure 1.28** Examples of subrange types

In Section 5, a recent change to Modula-2 is presented that allows a qualified identifier name to be used as an option in front of a subrange type.

## *Software Engineering:*

Subrange types allows a programmer to precisely express the allowable range of values for a given base type. The full power of the compiler and run-time environment can then serve the programmer in trapping illegal values.

# Structured Types

## Arrays

An array is a type constructor. A type constructor allows a programmer to build a given data structure from other data types.

The syntax of an array type is given as:

```
TYPE
    ident = ARRAY [ lowerlimit . . upperlimit ] OF type;
```

The elements of an array are all of the same base type. This may be any data type including another structured type. Each element in an array is distinguished from other elements by its index in the array.

In declaring an array, the index range of values is bracketed by a set of square brackets. Figure 1.29 shows some typical array-type declarations.

```
TYPE
    intvector   = ARRAY[ -10..10 ] OF INTEGER;
    truthtable  = ARRAY[ 1..100 ] OF BOOLEAN;
    lastname    = ARRAY[ 0..9 ] OF CHAR;
    namearray   = ARRAY[ 1..5 ] OF lastname;
    data        = ARRAY[ 1..10 ] OF ARRAY[ 1..100 ] OF
                  CARDINAL;
```

**Figure 1.29** Array-type declarations

The last array type in Figure 1.29 is an array of arrays. We could declare data as a two-dimensional array. Figure 1.30 shows data declared as a two-dimensional array.

```
TYPE data = ARRAY[ 1..10 ], [ 1..100 ] OF CARDINAL
```

**Figure 1.30** Two-dimensional array declaration

We may access the elements of an array as shown in Figure 1.31.

## *Hazard:*

A reference to a two-dimensional variable, such as d in Figure 1.31, with only one index is illegal. If a single index reference to a multidimensional array is desired, the multidimensional array must be declared as an array of arrays (such as variable names).

There is no limit on the number of dimensions that may be declared in a multidimensional array.

```
TYPE
    intvector  = ARRAY[ -10..10 ] OF INTEGER;
    truthtable = ARRAY[ 1..100 ] OF BOOLEAN;
    lastname   = ARRAY[ 0..9 ] OF CHAR;
    namearray  = ARRAY[ 1..5 ] OF lastname;
    data       = ARRAY[ 1..10 ], [ 1..100 ] OF CARDINAL;

VAR
    vector : intvector;
    table  : truthtable;
    name   : lastname;
    names  : namearray;
    d      : data;
```

```
vector[ -8 ]      accesses the integer in position -8.

table[ 99 ]       accesses the boolean variable position 99.

lastname[ 0 ]     accesses the first character of lastname.

name[ 5 ]         accesses the sixth character in name.

names[ 4 ]        accesses the 4th string in the array of
                  strings.

names[ 3 ][ 0 ]   accesses the first character of the 3rd
                  name.

d[ 3, 56 ]        accesses the third row and 56th column of
                  data.
```

**Figure 1.31** Accessing elements of an array

## *Hazard:*

In declaring multidimensional arrays, be aware that the size of the resulting structure may be prohibitively large. For example, if each real requires 8 bytes of storage, the size of the following structure is 200 million bytes.

```
VAR
    multidimensional : ARRAY[ 1..100 ], [ 1..50],
                       [ 1..10 ], [ 1..500] OF REAL;
```

## String

There is no formal string type in Modula-2. Strings may be constructed as an array of characters (see Arrays). The conditions that must be met in order for an array to qualify as a string are:

1.  The lower limit of the array is 0.

2.  The base type of the array is CHAR.

An example of a string of 10 characters, str, is:

```
VAR str : ARRAY[ 0..9 ] OF CHAR:
```

## *Hazard:*

If the lower limit of an array of characters is defined as 1 instead of 0,

```
VAR str : ARRAY [ 1..10 ] OF CHAR;
```

then procedures such as WriteString imported from library module InOut will fail (see InOut in Section 3).

## Records

A record is a type constructor. As indicated in connection with arrays, a type constructor allows a programmer to build a given data structure from other data types.

The syntax of a record type is given as:

```
TYPF
   ident = RECORD
             field1,
             field2 : type1;
             field3 : type2;
             . . .
           END(*record*);
```

The elements of a record are not necessarily of the same base type. Each element of a record may be an arbitrary data type, including another record.

The elements of a record, its fields, are accessed by using the record variable identifier followed by a dot, followed by the identifier name of the element (record field). The identifier (record variable name, dot, field name) is called a qualified

of qualification, the same field name may be
ord declarations.
ontain an arbitrary number of fields.
ows a typical record declaration and its
e demonstrates how complex information
ormed using type constructors.

```
r, rainy, snowy );

D
nth : [ 1..12 ];
y    : [ 1..31 ];
ar  : [ 0..2000 ];
* record *);

RD
timestamp : date;
hightemp,
lowtemp    : CARDINAL;
condition : weathercond;
END(* record *);
VAR
    data : ARRAY[ 1..365 ] OF weather;

data[ 121 ].timestamp.day - accesses the day number of
                            the 121st weather record

data[ 200 ].condition     - accesses the weather condition
                            of the 200th weather record

data[ 3 ].hightemp        - accesses the high temperature of
                            the 3rd weather record
```

**Figure 1.32** Record declarations

## *Style:*

It is recommended that the tabular layout shown in Figure 1.32
be used in record declarations. All the field identifiers should be
lined up, one beneath another. All the colons should line up. All
the field type identifiers should line up.

## *Hazard:*

In accessing records, it is common for inexperienced programmers to use the name of the record type rather than the name of
the record variable in the qualified identifier. For example, in
Figure 1.32 it would be incorrect to use.

```
weather [ 121 ].timestamp.day;
```

Figure 1.33 shows an array of records that contains an array within a record.

```
TYPE
    nametype = ARRAY[ 0..19 ] OF CHAR;

    infotype = RECORD
              name    : nametype;
              grades : ARRAY[ 1..5 ] OF REAL;
              END(* record *);
VAR
    rollbook : ARRAY[ 1..50 ] OF infotype;

rollbook[ 22 ].grades[ 4 ]  - accesses the 4th grade of the
                              22nd student

rollbook[ 18 ].name         - accesses the name of the 18th
                              student

rollbook[ 50 ].name[ 1 ]    - accesses the second letter of
                              the 50th student's name
```

**Figure 1.33** A record containing an array

## Variant Records

Variant records are used whenever a choice of data fields is desirable; that is, the set of data fields is not the same for all variant record variables.

The syntax of a variant record declaration is illustrated in Figure 1.34. Note that any number of record variants may be placed anywhere in a variant record.

Whenever an assignment is made to any field of a variant record, all other variants become undefined. The fields category and medical problem in Figure 1.34 are tag fields. The tag field of a variant record may be accessed like any regular field.

In statically allocating memory for a variant record declaration, the compiler allocates memory for the largest variant field of a variant record.

## *Software Engineering:*

In the past, particularly in Pascal, variant records have been used to affect type coercion (forcing a value of one data type to be interpreted as another data type). This is done by declaring a variant record in which the two fields, each of a different data type, require the same memory storage. An assignment is made to one of the data types and then the other data type is accessed.

```
TYPE

  nametype        = ARRAY[ 0..19 ] OF CHAR;

  employmentclass = ( permanent, temporary );

  infotype        = RECORD
                      name : nametype;
                      CASE category : employmentclass OF
                        permanent : yearlysalary : REAL; |
                        temporary : monthlywage  : REAL;
                      END(* case *);
                      CASE medicalproblem : BOOLEAN OF
                        TRUE  : doctorname : nametype;    |
                        FALSE :
                      END(* case *);
                      yearsonjob : CARDINAL;
                    END(* record *);
VAR
    database : ARRAY[ 1..1000 ] OF infotype;

database[ 300 ].yearlysalary - accesses the yearly salary of
                                the 300th record in the data
                                base
```

**Figure 1.34** Illustration of variant record

Strictly speaking, this represents a misuse of variant records. Fortunately, Modula-2 provides facilities for accomplishing type coercion directly. See type conversion and type transfer.

## Sets

A set is an unordered collection of elements chosen from some base or universe set. In Modula-2, the base set must be of a simple type, that is Boolean, character, integer, enumeration, or subrange. Each implementation of Modula-2 imposes limitations on the cardinality of the base type.

A predefined set in Modula-2 is the BITSET. Its allowable values are the set of all possible subsets of the integers { 0, 1, 2, ..., b − 1 }, where b is the number of bits in the memory word of the computer system.

BITSETS are in one-to-one correspondence to bitvectors, strings of binary 0's and 1's. The mapping from BITSETS to bitvectors is dependent on the byte sex of the machine (most significant byte on the right or left). Figure 1.35 repeats part of Figure 1.13 and shows the mapping between BITSETS and bitvectors for a 16-bit machine.

```
Set                          Bitvector
-------------------------------------
{}                           0000000000000000

{ 0, 1, 2 }                  0000000000000111

{ 1, 4, 9, 12, 15 }   1001001000010010
```

**Figure 1.35** Mapping between BITSETS and bitvectors

It is possible to declare different set types with the same or intersecting base types. To distinguish constants of the various set types, the type identifier of the set must precede the set bracket. Figure 1.36 illustrates this with some typical set declarations.

```
TYPE
    smallrange = [ 0..30 ];

    largerange = [ 0..500 ];

    set1       = SET OF smallrange;

    set2       = SET OF largerange;

    set1{ 10..20, 29, 30 }       - denotes elements from set1

    set2{ 10..20, 50, 475, 500 } - denotes elements from
                                     set2

    { 1, 4, 6, 8 }               - the absence of a type
                                     identifier denotes
                                     elements from a bitset
```

**Figure 1.36** Typical set declarations

The allowable operations on sets are inclusion, union, intersection, difference, and symmetric difference. Figure 1.37 shows the set operations and their symbols.

```
Set Operation        Symbol
-------------        ------

inclusion            IN
union                +
intersection         *
difference           -
symmetric difference /
```

**Figure 1.37** Set operations and their symbols

In Figure 1.38, the meanings of each set operation are given.

```
inclusion
---------
The IN operator is used to determine set membership.  For
example,

a IN set1{ 10..20, 29, 30 } returns true if a is a member of
this set, otherwise returns false.

union
-----
The union of two sets results in a set that contains all
elements that are in either operand set, or in both.

intersection
------------
The intersection of two sets results in a set that contains
only the elements that are in both operand sets.

difference
----------
The difference of two sets results in a set that contains
the elements of the first operand set that are not contained
in the second operand set.

symmetric difference
--------------------
The symmetric difference of two sets results in a set that
contains the elements that are in exactly one of the two
operand sets.
```

**Figure 1.38**  Meaning of set operations

Figure 1.39 illustrates each of the set operations.

```
union
-----
{} + { 1, 3, 4 } = { 1, 3, 4 }
{ 1, 3, 4 } + { 3, 5, 7 } = { 1, 3, 4, 5, 7 }

intersection
------------
{ 1, 3, 4, 5, 7 } * {} = {}
{ 1, 3, 4 } * { 3, 5, 7 } = { 3 }

difference
----------
{ 1, 2, 5, 8 } - { 2, 4, 6, 8 } = { 1, 5 }

symmetric difference
--------------------
{ 2, 6, 10 } / { 4, 6, 8 } = { 2, 4, 8, 10 }
{ 1, 2, 5 } / { 1, 2, 6 } = { 5, 6 }
```

**Figure 1.39**  Illustration of set operations

Two important predefined procedures that are defined for sets are INCL and EXCL. (See Predefined Functions and Procedures.)

## *Software Engineering:*

Set types are particularly useful in input/output statements. Suppose a menu-driven program prompts a user to input one of the characters 'A' through 'J.' The following set type declarations allows a program to perform simple error trapping for an illegal input response.

```
TYPE
   charset = SET OF CHAR;

VAR
   ch : CHAR;

read( ch ); (* Response to menu prompt. *)
IF ch IN charset{ 'A' .. 'J' }
THEN
   ...
ELSE
   (* error handling statements *)
```

Some implementations of Modula-2 limit the cardinality of set types to only 16 or 32 elements. On such systems it would be impossible to use the above code because the declaration, SET OF CHAR, exceeds the cardinality of set types. The solution to the problem is to simulate a large character set using the predefined BITSET construct. Figure 1.40 shows several procedures that may be used to construct a character set on a machine that limits the cardinality of ordinary sets to a small value.

```
CONST
        maxpiece  = 15;
        piecesize = 16;

TYPE
        piecerange = [ 0..maxpiece ];
        charset    = ARRAY[ 0 .. maxpiece ] OF BITSET;


PROCEDURE include
              ( VAR chset     : charset          (* in/out *);
                    ch        : CHAR             (* in     *) );
```

```
BEGIN
  IF ORD( ch ) < 128
  THEN
    INCL( chset[ ORD( ch ) DIV piecesize  ],
          ORD( ch ) MOD piecesize );
  END(* if then *);
END include;


PROCEDURE exclude
        ( VAR chset       : charset           (* in/out *);
              ch          : CHAR              (* in     *) );

BEGIN
  IF ORD( ch ) < 128
  THEN
    EXCL( chset[ ORD( ch ) DIV piecesize ],  ORD( ch ) MOD
          piecesize );
  END(* if then *);
END exclude;


PROCEDURE inset
        (     chset       : charset           (* in  *);
              ch          : CHAR              (* in  *) ) :
BOOLEAN;

BEGIN
  IF ORD( ch ) < 128
  THEN
    RETURN ORD(  ch  ) MOD piecesize IN chset[ ORD( ch )
                                        DIV piecesize  ];
  ELSE
    RETURN FALSE;
  END(* if then *);
END inset;


PROCEDURE union
        ( VAR chset3        : charset (* out *);
              chset1, chset2 : charset (* in  *) );

  VAR
      piece : piecerange;

BEGIN
  FOR piece := 0 TO maxpiece DO
    chset3[  piece  ] := chset1[  piece  ] +
                         chset2[  piece  ];
  END(* for loop *);
END union;


PROCEDURE intersection
          ( VAR chset3   : charset           (* out *);
                chset1   : charset           (* in *);
                chset2   : charset           (* in *) );
```

*(continued)*

```
      VAR
            piece : piecerange;
      BEGIN
        FOR piece := 0 TO maxpiece DO
          chset3[  piece  ] := chset1[  piece  ] *
                                    chset2[  piece  ];
        END(* for loop *);
      END intersection;
```

**Figure 1.40**  Procedures for constructing character set

## Files

Modula-2 does not have a file constructor. Each implementation of Modula-2 provides a file library with a complete set of file input/output procedures. (See Section 3.)

## Pointer Variables

A pointer is a type constructor. Every pointer is bound to another data type called the base type. The base type of a pointer may be any data type, either predefined or programmer defined.

A pointer is a memory address that contains the starting address of the base type pointed to. Pointers are assignment compatible with address variables. (See ADDRESS type.)

The set of allowable values for the pointer is the set of memory addresses of objects of the base type.

The syntax of a pointer type is given as:

```
    TYPF
      ident = POINTER TO basetype;
```

Figure 1.41 illustrates pointer declarations.

Figure 1.41 shows treenode declared in terms of node; but at the point of declaration, node has not yet been defined. Furthermore, the fields left and right of record type node are defined in terms of type treenode.

Modula-2 allows pointer types to be defined recursively. This is the only Modula-2 type which may be constructed in terms of a type that is yet to be defined. The compiler checks to make sure the unknown type is later defined within the same block. If it isn't, a compiler error message is emitted.

```
TYPE

    vector       = ARRAY[ 1..1000 ] OF CARDINAL;

    realpointer  = POINTER TO REAL;

    treenode     = POINTER TO node;

    node         = RECORD
                       info  : INTEGER;
                       left  : treenode;
                       right : treenode;
                   END(* record *);

    arrayptr     = POINTER TO vector;
```

**Figure 1.41** Pointer declarations

Memory sufficient to store one memory address is statically allocated when a pointer variable is declared, regardless of the size of the base type. Memory space for the base type may be dynamically allocated (at runtime) using one of two standard procedures, NEW or ALLOCATE. Memory space for the base type may be dynamically deallocated using one of two standard procedures, DISPOSE or DEALLOCATE.

Standard procedures ALLOCATE and DEALLOCATE must be imported from module Storage. The programmer may wish to write his or her own memory management procedures and use them in place of the above procedures.

Figure 1.42 shows the procedure interface to the memory management procedures NEW, ALLOCATE, DISPOSE, and DEALLOCATE. (See Procedures and Procedure Functions.)

When NEW is applied to a pointer that points to a variant record, another form of NEW and DISPOSE is sometimes available. Additional parameters are supplied indicating the values of the tag fields that specify the variants desired. For specific details, check your particular implementation of module Storage.

The only allowable operations on pointer types are the dereferencing operator, a unary postfix operator, ˆ, and assignment. The dereferencing operator, ˆ, is used to access the base type pointed to by a pointer variable.

Pointer variables are said to be anonymous variables because they are actually memory addresses that permit access to a base type through the dereferencing operator.

```
PROCEDURE ALLOCATE
        ( VAR a     : ADDRESS  (* out *);
              size : CARDINAL (* in *) );
(* Memory of size bytes is allocated starting at address a.
                                                          *)


PROCEDURE DEALLOCATE
        ( VAR a     : ADDRESS  (* out *);
              size : CARDINAL (* in *) );
(* Memory of size bytes is deallocated starting at address
    a.                                                    *)


PROCEDURE NEW
        ( VAR p : ADDRESS (* out *) );
(* Memory of size equal to the base type pointed to by p is
    allocated starting at address p.                      *)


PROCEDURE DISPOSE
        ( VAR p : ADDRESS (* out *) );
(* Memory of size equal to the base type pointed to by p is
    deallocated starting at address p.                    *)
```

**Figure 1.42**  Interface to procedures ALLOCATE, DEALLOCATE, NEW, and DISPOSE

Figure 1.43 illustrates pointer variables and the dereference operator.

Figure 1.44 graphically depicts pointer type treenode.

## Constant NIL

The predefined constant, NIL, is a member of the value set of any pointer variable. Indeed, NIL is a unique memory reference that may not be assigned by the memory management procedures NEW or ALLOCATE. NIL is used as a sentinel for dynamic data structures such as lists and trees because it is a unique memory address.

## *Hazard: Aliasing effects*

Aliasing occurs when an operation on one pointer causes a fallout effect on another pointer.

The following short program segment illustrates aliasing of pointers, a serious hazard when programming with pointers.

Suppose the programmer's intention is to assign a value to the location pointed to by b that is equal to the value pointed to by a. The following erroneous program segment, Figure 1.45, attempts to do this.

```
TYPE

    vector      = ARRAY[ 1..1000 ] OF CARDINAL;

    realpointer = POINTER TO REAL;

    treenode    = POINTER TO node;

    node        = RECORD
                     info  : INTEGER;
                     left  : treenode;
                     right : treenode;
                  END(* record *);

    arrayptr    = POINTER TO vector;

VAR

    realptr : realpointer;

    tree    : treenode;

    data    : arrayptr;

    rec     : ARRAY[ -100..100 ] OF treenode;
```

```
realptr^            - contains a real value with address
                      realptr

tree^.info          - contains the integer value contained in
                      the record with address tree

tree^.left          - contains the address of another treenode
                      record

tree^.left.info     - contains the integer value contained in
                      the record pointed to by the left field
                      of record tree^

data^[ 56 ]         - contains the cardinal value of the 56th
                      element of the array pointed to by data

rec[ -70 ]^.info    - contains the integer value contained in
                      the -70th record element in the array rec
```

**Figure 1.43**  Examples of the dereference operator

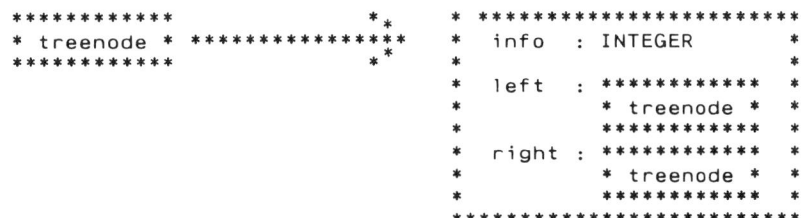

**Figure 1.44**  Graphical depiction of treenode

```
VAR
    a, b : POINTER TO INTEGER;

NEW( a ); (* Dynamically allocates memory space for an
              integer.                                    *)
a^ := -20; (* The value pointed to by a is assigned -20.  *)
NEW( b ) ; (* Dynamically allocates memory space for an
              integer.                                    *)
b := a;    (* Pointer b has the address of a and points to
              the value -20.                              *)
WriteInt( b^, 5 ); (* The value -20 is output.            *)
a^ := 17;
WriteInt( b^, 5 ); (* The value 17 is output because of
                      aliasing.                           *)
```

**Figure 1.45** Erroneous program segment illustrating aliasing

When the value pointed to by a is assigned the new value 17, the value pointed to by b is also changed to 17 even though the programmer wanted this value to be − 20.

The offending line of code is,

    b := a;

This is a strong assignment statement forcing pointers b and a to represent the same memory address.

The correct, in this case weaker, assignment statement is,

    b^ := a^;

This assignment statement assigns the value pointed to by a to the value pointed to by b. The address of pointers a and b are not the same. When a^ is reassigned a new value, the value of b^ is not changed.

## Hazard: Dangling pointer

It is the responsibility of the programmer to deallocate all memory storage that is dynamically allocated when the information stored in this memory is no longer needed. The program segment given in Figure 1.46 illustrates how poor pointer variable management may result in memory that is inaccessible and thus useless. This phenomenon is referred to as a dangling pointer. The program segment in Figure 1.46 dynamically creates three records containing the information 16, 24, and 18.

When pointer variable data is dynamically deallocated, the pointer to the second record is destroyed; therefore, the information contained in this second record is no longer accessible.

```
TYPE
    list = POINTER TO node;
    node = RECORD
              info : CARDINAL;
              next : list;
           END(* record *);

VAR
    data : list;
    temp : list;
    loc  : list;

NEW( data ); (* Dynamically allocates memory for a record of
                type node.                                    *)
data^.info := 16;
NEW( temp ); (* Dynamically allocates memory for a record of
                type temp.                                    *)
temp^.info := 24;
data^.next := temp; (* Record data "points" to record temp.
                                                              *)
NEW( loc ); (* Dynamically allocates memory for a record of
                type loc.                                     *)
loc^.info := 18;
temp^.next := loc; (* Record temp "points" to record loc. *)
temp := loc; (* The address of temp is reassigned to equal
                the address of loc.                           *)
DISPOSE( data );
```

**Figure 1.46** Program segment that illustrates a dangling pointer

The memory of this second record is said to "dangle." Although space is occupied by this second record information, the information is useless to us.

## *Hazard: Uninitialized pointers*

Perhaps one of the most common and serious errors committed by inexperienced programmers is the failure to initialize the value of one or more pointer variables. The mere declaration of a pointer variable does not imply the initialization of the pointer variable to a memory address. Figure 1.47 shows a program segment that illustrates this problem.

```
VAR
    arrayptr : POINTER TO ARRAY[ 1..2 ] OF REAL;

arrayptr^[ 1 ] := -234.6;
arrayptr^[ 2 ] := 7772.9;
```

**Figure 1.47** Example of an uninitialized pointer

In Figure 1.47, the pointer variable arrayptr, before it is assigned a memory address, may point to anything in the memory set of the computer. With poor luck, arrayptr may point to an important section of the disk operating system information. By assigning 16 bytes to arrayptr^[ 1 ] and arrayptr^[ 2 ] (we assume 8-byte reals), we may inadvertently overwrite a critical section of the disk operating system and find that our computer is crippled.

What makes uninitialized pointers particularly difficult to detect is that the compiler provides no help in trapping such errors. It is the complete responsibility of the programmer to guard against such errors.

The two ways to initialize a pointer variable are:

1.   Use a NEW or ALLOCATE operation on the pointer.

2.   Assign to the pointer another pointer or NIL.

## *Software Engineering:*

The most common and perhaps important application of pointer variables is in the construction of dynamic data structures such as stacks, queues, lists, and trees. Figure 1.48 shows the code for a dynamic stack structure implemented with the use of pointer variables. Note how the constant NIL is used as a sentinel in the linked list used to implement a stack. (See Procedures and Procedure functions. See Expressions.)

```
TYPE

    elementtype = CARDINAL;

    stack       = POINTER TO stacknode;

    stacknode   = RECORD
                      item  :   elementtype;
                      next  :   stack;
                  END(* record *);

PROCEDURE define
        ( VAR s : stack  (* out *) );
(* Initializes the stack to the empty state.              *)

BEGIN
  s := NIL
END define;


PROCEDURE makeempty
        ( VAR s : stack   (* in/out *) );
(* Takes an initialized stack and deallocates all memory
   storage leaving the stack in an empty state.           *)

VAR
  p : stack;
```

```
BEGIN
  WHILE ( s # NIL ) DO
    p := s;
    s := s^.next;
    DISPOSE( p );
  END (* while loop *)
END makeempty;


PROCEDURE empty
          (    s : stack (* in *) ) : BOOLEAN;
(* Returns true if the stack is empty, otherwise false.   *)

BEGIN
  RETURN ( s = NIL );
END empty;


PROCEDURE push
          ( VAR s    : stack       (* in/out *);
                item : elementtype (* in *) );
(* Adds item to the stack s.                              *)

VAR
  p : stack;

BEGIN
  NEW( p );
  p^.next := s;
  p^.item := item;
  s := p
END push;


PROCEDURE stackunderflow;

(* Error handling procedure:  message, recovery, abort, etc.*)
BEGIN
  ...
END stackunderflow;


PROCEDURE pop
          ( VAR s    : stack       (* in/out *);
            VAR item : elementtype (* out *) );
(* Removes the item from the stack s.                     *)

VAR
  p : stack;

BEGIN
  IF empty( s )
  THEN
    stackunderflow
  ELSE
    p := s;
    item := s^.item;
    s := s^.next;
    DISPOSE( p );
  END (* if then *);
END pop;
```

*(continued)*

```
PROCEDURE topofstack
         (    s : stack  (* in *) ) : elementtype;
BEGIN
  IF empty( s )
  THEN
    stackunderflow
  ELSE
    RETURN s^.item
  END (* if then *)
END topofstack;
```

**Figure 1.48** Dynamic stack structure

A stack is an ordered collection of items in which the insertion of a new item or the removal of an existing item can be made at only one end, called the top of the stack. A stack is often referred to as a last-in, first-out (or LIFO) list.

# Expressions

## Relational Operators

Relational operators may be applied to all scalar types (Boolean, cardinal, character, enumeration, integer, real, and subrange). They are used to compare the values of scalar data objects (variables). The six relational operators are given in Figure 1.49.

```
Operator                   Symbol
---------------------------------

equal                      =
not equal (inequality)     # or <>
greater than               >
less than                  <
greater than or equal      >=
less than or equal         <=
```

**Figure 1.49** Relational operators

Each of the relational operators returns a Boolean value when applied to two operands.

The equality and inequality operators may be applied to pointer types. The other four relational operators cannot be applied to pointer types.

All of the operators except $>$ and $<$ may be applied to set types. (See Set.) The meaning of $\geq$ is superset, and the meaning of $\leq$ is subset.

The relational operators may not be applied to any structured data types.

## *Hazard:*

It is common for inexperienced programmers to attempt to compare two arrays as follows:

```
TYPE vector = ARRAY[ 1..100 ] OF INTEGER;

VAR
  a, b : vector;

IF a = b
THEN
   ...
```

Such a comparison is illegal. It would be equally illegal to compare two records or to write

```
IF a > b
THEN
   ...
```

## Operator Precedence

All operators in Modula-2 are given a precedence that allows the unambiguous evaluation of expressions regardless of the presence of parentheses. Figure 1.50 shows the hierarchy of operator precedence.

```
unary +, unary -, NOT

*, /, DIV, MOD, AND, &, * (sets), / (sets)

+, -, OR, + (sets), - ( sets )

=, <>, #, <, <=, >, >=, IN, <= (sets) >= (sets).
```

**Figure 1.50**  Hierarchy of operator precedence

In the case of two operators of equal precedence, the order of evaluation proceeds from left to right.

*Hazard:*

The following expression is incorrect:

$-20 \leq$ value AND value $< 50$;

It is evident from Figure 1.50 that the precedence of the operator AND is higher than the precedence of the relational operator $\leq$ or $<$. Thus the compiler attempts to evaluate value AND value. This is impossible because value is not a Boolean expression (an expression that evaluates to TRUE or FALSE).

The correct form for the expression is:

$(-20 \leq$ value $)$ AND $($ value $< 50 )$;

Figure 1.51 shows some expressions and their values.

```
Expression              Value when a = 2.0, b = 3.0, c = 4.0
------------------------------------------------------------

a * b + c                              10.0

a * ( b + c )                          14.0

a + b * c                              14.0

a * b / c + a                           3.5

a * b / c * a                           3.0
```

**Figure 1.51** Expressions and their values

## Assignment Compatibility

The strong type checking feature of a Modula-2 compiler constrains the left side of an assignment statement to be of the same type as the right side of such an assignment statement.

In order for one variable to be assigned to another, the two variables must be assignment compatible. Figure 1.52 lists the rules for assignment compatibility in Modula-2.

Figure 1.53 presents an example to illustrate assignment compatibility and incompatibility.

Two variables v1 and v2 are assignment compatible if and only if one of the following conditions is true:

1.  v1 and v2 are of the same non-anonymous type.

2.  v1 and v2 are defined in terms of types that have been equated.  An example of a type equation is:

    ```
    TYPE a = CARDINAL;
         b = a;
    ```

3.  v1 is a subrange of v2 or v2 is a subrange of v1.

4.  v1 and v2 are both subranges of the same type.

5.  v1 is an integer or subrange of integers, v2 is a cardinal or a subrange of cardinal or vice-versa.

6.  v1 and v2 are string types ( ARRAY[ 0..upperlimit ] ) and the length of the string on the left-side of the assignment statement is at least as great as the string on the right-side of the assignment statement.

**Figure 1.52**  Rules for assignment compatibility

```
TYPE
     singledigit  = [ 0..9 ];

     doubledigit  = [ 10..99 ];

     tripledigit  = [ 100..999 ];

     smallnumbers = ARRAY[ 1..10 ] OF singledigit;

     largenumbers = ARRAY[ 1..20 ] OF tripledigit;

VAR
     small : singledigit;
     large : tripledigit;
     snum  : smallnumbers;
     lnum  : largenumbers;
     large : ARRAY[ 1..20 ] OF CARDINAL;

BEGIN
  small := snum[ 9 ];
  large := lnum[ 2 ];
  small := 4;
  small := large; (* Although this statement is syntatically
                     correct, it will produce a run-time
                     range error.                          *)

     We list some illegal assignment statements:

  lnum := large;  - lnum is of a different type than large.
  snum := lnum;   - snum is of a different type than lnum.
```

**Figure 1.53**  Example of assignment compatibility

## *Software Engineering:*

A programmer should exploit the fact that record variables of the same type may be assigned to each other and that array variables of the same type may be assigned to each other. The following loop assignment of the two arrays a and b may be replaced by the simple assignment statement,

```
                                          a := b;

TYPE
     vector = ARRAY[ 1..10000 ] OF REAL;

VAR
     a, b : vector;
     i    : CARDINAL;

FOR i := 1 TO 10000 DO
  a[ i ] := b[ i ];
END(* for loop *);
```

The following record assignment of the two record variables a and b may be replaced by the simple assignment statement,

```
                                          a := b;

TYPE
     datatype =
     RECORD
       info      : CARDINAL;
       age       : REAL;
       lastname  : ARRAY[ 0..9 ] OF CHAR;
       firstname : ARRAY[ 0..9 ] OF CHAR;
     END(* record *);

VAR
     a, b : datatype;
     i    : CARDINAL;

a.info := b.info;
a.age := b.age;
FOR i := 0 TO 9 DO
  a.lastname[ i ] := b.lastname[ i ];
  a.firstname[ i ] := b.firstname[ i ];
END(* for loop *);
```

# Type Conversion and Type Transfer

Type conversion changes a value from one type to another by changing the internal representation.

Type transfer changes a value from one type to another by maintaining the internal representation but changing the interpretation. Because the internal representation is not changed using type transfer, the argument and image must be of the same size.

There are two type conversion functions predefined in Modula-2, TRUNC and FLOAT.

TRUNC( r ) takes a real argument, r, and converts it to a cardinal result. FLOAT( c ) takes a cardinal argument, c, and converts it to a real result.

Figure 1.54 shows some type conversions.

```
VAR
    card    : CARDINAL;
    number  : CARDINAL;
    average : REAL;
    sum     : REAL;

(* We simulate the round function *)
card := TRUNC( FLOAT( card ) + 0.5 );

average := sum / FLOAT( number );
```

**Figure 1.54** Some type conversions

The predefined functions ORD and CHR are type transfer functions.

The function ORD is defined on Boolean, cardinal, integer, and all enumeration types. It returns a value that represents the position in the value set of the type of its parameter. Its value on negative integer parameters is undefined.

The function VAL is defined on Boolean, cardinal, integer, and all enumeration types. It requires two parameters, the first being a type identifier and the second an ordinal value. It returns an enumeration constant associated with the ordinal value.

Figure 1.55 illustrates the use of the ORD and VAL functions.

The type identifier of any type may be used to transfer the value of any other type of the same size into that type. It is often necessary to convert integer types to cardinal or cardinal types to integers as in Figure 1.56.

```
TYPE
        weekdays = ( Mon, Tues, Wed, Thurs, Fri );

VAR
        flag : BOOLEAN;
        day  : weekdays;
        ch   : CHAR;
        card : CARDINAL;

flag := FALSE;
card := ORD( flag );            (* card = 0       *)
flag := VAL( BOOLEAN, 1 );      (* flag = TRUE    *)
day  := VAL( weekdays, 3 );     (* day = Thurs    *)
DEC( day, 2 );                  (* day = Tues     *)
ch := VAL( CHAR, 67 );          (* ch = 'C'       *)
ch := CHR( 67 );                (* ch = 'C'       *)
card := ORD( day );             (* card = 1       *)
card := ORD( ch );              (* card = 67      *)
```

**Figure 1.55** ORD and VAL type transfer functions

```
VAR
    c : CARDINAL;
    i : INTEGER;

i := -30 + INTEGER( c );
IF i >= 0
THEN
   c := 60 + CARDINAL( i );
END(* if then *);
```

**Figure 1.56** Type transfer between integer and cardinal

Figure 1.57 illustrates type transfers that are built using programmer-defined types.

```
TYPE
     str1 = ARRAY[ 0..7 ] OF CHAR;
     str2 = ARRAY[ 1..2 ] OF CHAR;

VAR
     r  : REAL;
     c  : CARDINAL;
     s1 : str1;
     s2 : str2;

r := 1.2345;  (* We assume an 8 byte representation.     *)
s1 := str1( r ); (* The bit pattern of r is interpreted as a
                    string.                               *)
s2 := "CD";
c := CARDINAL( s2 ); (* The bit pattern of string s2 is
                        interpreted as a cardinal.        *)
s2 := str2( TRUNC( r ) );
```

**Figure 1.57** Type transfers using programmer-defined types

## *Hazard:*

The most common error in using type transfers is the failure to ensure that the size of the parameter in the type transfer matches the size of the image type. For example, on a machine such as an IBM PC in which an address is 4 bytes and a cardinal is 2 bytes, the following type transfer would be in error:

```
VAR
   card: CARDINAL;
   adr : ADDRESS;

   card := CARDINAL( adr ); (* Erroneous type transfer *)
```

# Predefined Functions and Procedures

Figure 1.58 lists the predefined procedures and functions of Modula-2.

ABS( n ) returns the negative of the number n if n < 0 and returns n if n ≥ 0.

INC and DEC take two forms. The first form involves one argument, the number that we wish to increment or decrement, as illustrated here.

```
INC( n ) → n := n + 1
DEC( n ) → n := n − 1
```

```
ABS    - Absolute value, operates on all numeric types.

INC    - Increment, operates on integer and cardinal types.

DEC    - Decrement, operates on integer and cardinal types.

ODD    - Odd, operates on the cardinal type.

CAP    - Uppercase, operates on the character type.

ORD    - Ordinal, operates on character types and other
         enumeration types.

VAL    - Value, operates on character types and other
         enumeration types.

TRUNC  - Truncation, operates on the real type.

FLOAT  - Operates on integer and cardinal types.

INCL   - Include, operates on the set type.

EXCL   - Exclude, operates on the set type.
```

**Figure 1.58** Predefined functions and procedures

The second form of INC and DEC involves two arguments, the number that we wish to increment or decrement and the amount that we wish to increment or decrement.

```
INC( n, amt ) → n : = n + amt
DEC( n, amt ) → n : = n − amt
```

ODD( n ) returns TRUE if the cardinal n is an even number; otherwise, it returns FALSE.

CAP( ch ) returns the upper-case equivalent of the character ch if ch is a lower-case character ('a' .. 'z'), and leaves ch unchanged if ch is not a lower-case character.

ORD( ch ) returns the cardinal code for the character ch. We assume that the coding of characters is given by the American Standard Code for Information Interchange (ASCII). (See Character.) For example, the ORD( 'A' ) = 65 and ORD( 'z' ) = 122.

ORD may also operate on an enumeration type. In such a case it returns the position, starting at 0, in the enumeration list. For example, for

```
trafficlighttype = ( red, amber, green ),
```

then if

```
trafficlight : = red, ORD( trafficlight ) = 0.
```

VAL is the inverse of ORD. As an example,

```
VAL( trafficlight, 2 ) = green.
```

In general

```
VAL( T, ORD( x ) ) = x
```

where T is an enumeration type.

TRUNC is a type conversion function that converts a variable of type real to a value of type cardinal. (See Type Conversion and Type Transfer.) For example,

```
TRUNC( 1.01 ) = 1,   TRUNC( 1.99 ) = 1
```

FLOAT is a type conversion function that converts a variable of type cardinal or integer to a value of type real. (See Type Conversion and Type Transfer.) For example,

```
FLOAT( 4 ) = 4.0,   FLOAT( 17 ) = 17.0.
```

INCL and EXCL are used to add or subtract an element from a set. For example,

```
INCL( charset, 'A' )
```

adds the character 'A' to charset.

```
EXCL( charset, 'D' )
```

removes the character 'D' from charset.

## Sequence Control Structures

Program execution in Modula-2, like most modern languages, proceeds from one statement to another, in sequence. Only when a loop structure or branching structure intervenes is the flow of control broken.

## Branching Structures

Branching structures provide facilities for a program to select one statement or group of statements from several alternatives for execution.

### IF THEN Statement

The IF THEN construct is perhaps the most widely used and important branching structure. An IF THEN statement is constructed as indicated in Figure 1.59.

```
IF boolean expression
THEN
   statement(s);
END(* if then *);
```

**Figure 1.59** IF THEN construct

The IF THEN construct is called a conditional branching structure because the statements between the THEN and END are either executed or not executed, depending on the value of the Boolean expression.

Some typical IF THEN statements are shown in Figure 1.60.

```
VAR
    a, b, c, d : CARDINAL;
    flag       : BOOLEAN;

flag := a > b;
IF ( flag ) OR ( c < d )
THEN
  WriteString( "We are in path 1." );
  d := 16;
END(* if then *);
```

**Figure 1.60**  Typical IF THEN statements

## Style:

There are many format conventions that may be used in writing an IF THEN statement. To promote readability, it is suggested that the body of code that is executed between the THEN and END statements be indented several spaces from the outer shell of the control structure. The style adopted here is to include the THEN statement on a separate line. This allows a comment that indicates the purpose of the indented code to be included, if appropriate, next to the THEN statement.

## IF THEN ELSE Statement

The IF THEN ELSE statement is constructed as shown in Figure 1.61.

```
IF boolean expression
THEN
  statement(s);
ELSE
  statement(s);
  END(* if then *);
```

**Figure 1.61**  The IF THEN ELSE construct

The IF THEN ELSE statement is called a two-way branching structure because one of two blocks of code are executed depending on the value of a Boolean expression.

Some typical IF THEN ELSE statements are shown in Figure 1.62.

```
VAR
    a, b, c, d : INTEGER;

IF ( 2 * a - b * c > d ) AND ( d > -50 )
THEN
  WriteString( "We are in branch 1." );
  d := 46;
  a := 24;
ELSE
  WriteString( "We are in branch 2." );
  d := -24;
  a := -11;
END(* if then *);
```

**Figure 1.62**  Typical IF THEN ELSE statements

## *Style:*

The semicolons in the statements just above the ELSE and END are optional. The style adopted here is to use the semicolons so that if additional lines of code are later added after these statements, a missing semicolon will not result.

As with the IF THEN construct, a separate line is used for the THEN and ELSE statements to provide space for an optional comment that describes the purpose of the indented block of code.

## IF THEN ELSIF ELSE Statement

The IF THEN ELSIF ELSE statement is constructed as shown in Figure 1.63.

The IF THEN ELSIF ELSE statement is called a multiway branch because one of several blocks of code is executed depending on the result of possibly several Boolean expressions.

Some typical IF THEN ELSIF ELSE statements are shown in Figure 1.64.

```
IF boolean expression1
THEN
   statement(s);
ELSIF boolean expression2
THEN
   statement(s);
ELSIF boolean expression3 (* optional *)
THEN
   statement(s);
(* additional optional ELSIF statements *)
ELSE (* optional *)
   statement(s);
END(* if then *);
```

**Figure 1.63** IF THEN ELSE construct

```
VAR
    ch1, ch2, ch3, ch4 : CHAR;
    a, b               : CARDINAL;

IF ch1 = ch2
THEN
  a := 6;
  b := 7;
ELSIF ch2 < ch4
THEN
  a := 17;
  b := 2;
ELSIF ( ( ch3 <= ch4 ) OR ( ch1 >= ch2 ) ) AND ( ch4 = 'Z' )
THEN
  a := 21;
  b := 0;
ELSE
  a := 1200;
  b := 1500;
END(* if then *);
```

**Figure 1.64** Some typical IF THEN ELSE statements

## *Style:*

As with the IF THEN and IF THEN ELSE constructs, a separate line is used for the THEN, ELSIF and ELSE statements to provide space for an optional comment that describes the purpose of the indented block of code.

## *Software Engineering:*

Because of the short-circuiting of Boolean expressions, great care must be exercised in setting up the Boolean expressions that comprise branching control structures. For example, the implication of the structure

```
IF (b > 0) AND (c ≥ a/b)
THEN
    ...
```

is different from the structure

```
IF ( c ≥ a / b ) AND ( b > 0 )
THEN
   ...
```

The first structure is preferred because it prevents a divide-by-zero error from occurring.

## CASE Statement

The case statement provides another way to achieve a multiway branch (a selection among several alternatives) in a program. A case statement is constructed as shown in Figure 1.65.

```
CASE selector OF
  alternative(s) 1 : statement(s);      |
  alternative(s) 2 : statement(s);      |
  ...
  alternative(s) j : statement(s);
ELSE (* optional *)
  statement(s);
END(* case *);
```

**Figure 1.65** Case construct

The selector in the case statement is an expression of a scalar type. Each of the alternatives are associated with possible values of the expression. The selector cannot be a real type.

Figure 1.66 shows an example of a case statement.

The case statement is also used in variant record declarations. (See Variant Records under Records.)

## *Hazard:*

It is the programmer's responsibility to ensure that every possible value of the case selector expression is accounted for in the case alternatives. The ELSE block of code may be used to account for all other contingencies. If the case selector expression has a value not given in one of the case alternatives and an ELSE statement is not provided, a severe run-time crash will occur.

```
VAR
     selector : CARDINAL;
     a, b, c  : INTEGER;

CASE ( 3 * selector + 10 ) OF
   0 .. 50 :
     a := -10;
     b := -5;
     c := -20;                    |
   51, 52  :
     a := -5;
     b := 0;
     c := 4;                      |
   53 .. 100, 105 :
     a := 0;
     b := 2;
     c := -55;                    |
   106 .. 1000
     a := 0;
     b := 0;
     c := 0;
ELSE
   WriteString( "Data error." );
END(* case *);
```

**Figure 1.66** A typical case statement

## *Software Engineering:*

The case statement has been used frequently to convert a numeral to a cardinal number as shown in Figure 1.67.

```
CASE ch OF
   '0' : number := 0;   |
   '1' : number := 1;   |
   '2' : number := 2;   |
   '3' : number := 3;   |
   '4' : number := 4;   |
   '5' : number := 5;   |
   '6' : number := 6;   |
   '7' : number := 7;   |
   '8' : number := 8;   |
   '9' : number := 9
ELSE
   WriteString( "Error in character." );
END(* case *);
```

**Figure 1.67** Case statement to convert numeral to number

A more efficient way to convert a numeral to a number is given in Figure 1.68.

```
IF ( ORD( ch ) >= ORD( '0' ) ) AND
   ( ORD( ch ) <= ORD( '9' ) )
THEN
   number := ORD( ch ) - ORD( '0' );
END(* if then *);
```

**Figure 1.68** More efficient conversion from numeral to number

# Iterative Structures

Iterative structures, loops, allow a program to execute a statement or group of statements more than once, subject to a condition or conditions that specify when the execution is to terminate.

## WHILE loop

A WHILE loop is constructed as shown in Figure 1.69.

```
WHILE boolean expression DO
   statement(s);
END(* while loop *);
```

**Figure 1.69** WHILE loop

The Boolean expression enables us to perform a test before we enter the loop to see whether we should enter the loop. When the Boolean expression is FALSE, we transfer control to the line directly beneath the END statement of the loop.

The WHILE loop is an example of a top-testing loop. A Boolean expression must evaluate to TRUE before each iteration of the loop.

Figure 1.70 displays code segments using WHILE loops for computing the sum of values in an array and for computing the number of values greater than 100 in an array.

```
VAR
     index, sum : CARDINAL;
     count      : CARDINAL;
     list       : ARRAY[ 1..1000 ] OF CARDINAL;

index := 1;
sum   := 0;
(* Sum of values stored in sum.                    *)
WHILE index <= 1000 DO
  sum := sum + list[ index ];
  index := index + 1;
END(* while loop *);

count := 0;
index := 1;
(* number of values > 100 stored in count.         *)
WHILE ( index <= 1000 ) DO
  IF list[ index ] > 100
  THEN
    INC( count );
  END(* if then *);
  INC( index );
END(* while loop *);
```

**Figure 1.70** Example of WHILE loop

Figure 1.71 shows the code segment, using a WHILE loop, for searching for an integer key in an array of integers.

```
VAR
    found : BOOLEAN;
    index : CARDINAL;
    pos   : CARDINAL;
    a     : ARRAY[ 1..1000 ] OF CARDINAL;
    key   : CARDINAL;

found := FALSE;
index := 1;
pos := 0;
(* Answer found in pos.                                      *)
WHILE ( NOT found ) AND ( index <= 1000 ) DO
  IF a[ index ] = key
  THEN
    found := TRUE;
    pos := index;
  END(* if then *);
  INC( index );
END(* while loop *);
```

**Figure 1.71** Another example of WHILE loop

## *Style:*

The body of a loop, whether it contains a single statement or a group of statements, should be indented from the outer shell of the loop. This makes it much easier to see the block of code that is to be repeated.

## *Hazard:*

A common programming error in using WHILE loops is the "off-by-one" error. Such an error is caused by miscalculating the Boolean expression that terminates the loop. A typical "off-by-one" error is shown in Figure 1.72. The sum of values in the array a[] does not include the value a[ size ]. The index i is off by one.

```
VAR
    a   : ARRAY[ 1..size ] OF CARDINAL;
    i   : CARDINAL;
    sum : CARDINAL;

sum := 0;
i := 1;
WHILE ( i < size ) DO
  sum := sum + a[ i ];
  INC( i );
END(* while loop *);
```

**Figure 1.72** Off-by-one error

## REPEAT Loop

A REPEAT loop is constructed as shown in Figure 1.73.

```
REPEAT
   statement(s);
UNTIL ( boolean expression );
```

**Figure 1.73** REPEAT loop

Figure 1.74 displays some typical REPEAT loops.

The Boolean expression enables us to perform a test after we complete the loop to see whether we should leave the loop. When the Boolean expression is TRUE, we transfer control to the line directly beneath the UNTIL statement of the loop.

The repeat loop is an example of a bottom-testing loop. The loop must be executed once before a Boolean expression is evaluated to determine whether additional iterations are possible.

```
VAR
      i : CARDINAL;

i := 1;
REPEAT
  WriteCard( i, 1 );
  WriteLn;
  INC( i );
UNTIL i = 100;

TYPE color = ( red, blue, green, black, brown, orange );

VAR
    c : color;

c := red;
i := 0;
REPEAT
  INC( c );
  INC( i );
UNTIL c = brown;
WriteCard( i, 1 );
```

**Figure 1.74** Typical REPEAT loops

Figure 1.75 illustrates a practical application of REPEAT loops by writing a procedure that compares two strings alphabetically. We define string1 as greater than string2 in the usual alphabetical sense (apple < butter, apple < apples, etc.). (See Procedures and Procedure Functions. See RETURN.)

```
CONST upperlimit = xxx; (* Some appropriate value *)

TYPE string      = ARRAY[ 0..upperlimit ] OF CHAR;


PROCEDURE strequal
         (     str1, str2 : string (* in *) ) : BOOLEAN;

VAR
     len1,
     len2                : INTEGER;
     i                   : INTEGER;

BEGIN
  (* The procedure Length is imported from Strings.  See
     section 4, typical Modula-2 libraries.              *)
  len1 := Length(  str1  );
  len2 := Length(  str2  );
  IF len1 # len2
  THEN
    RETURN FALSE;
  ELSE
    i  := -1;
    REPEAT
      INC(  i  );
    UNTIL ( i = len1 - 1 ) OR ( str1[ i ] # str2[ i ] );
    RETURN str1[  i  ] = str2[  i  ];
  END(* if then *);
END strequal;


PROCEDURE strlessthan;
         (     str1, str2 : string (* in *) ) : BOOLEAN;

VAR
     len1,
     len2                : INTEGER;
     minlength           : INTEGER;
     i                   : INTEGER;

BEGIN
  len1 := Length(  str1  );
  len2 := Length(  str2  );
  IF len1 < len2
  THEN
    minlength := len1;
  ELSE
    minlength := len2;
  END(* if then *);
  i  := -1;
  REPEAT
    INC(  i  );
  UNTIL ( i = minlength - 1 ) OR ( str1[ i ] # str2[ i ] );
  IF str1[  i  ] = str2[  i  ]
  THEN
    RETURN len1 < len2;
  ELSE
    RETURN str1[  i  ] < str2[  i  ];
  END(* if then *);
END strlessthan;
```

**Figure 1.75**  String comparison using REPEAT loops

## Software Engineering:

What is the relationship between WHILE loops which are top-testing loops and REPEAT loops which are bottom-testing loops? The WHILE loop is the more general loop structure. This relationship is illustrated in Figure 1.76.

```
While Loop                        Equivalent Repeat Loop
----------                        ----------------------

WHILE boolean expression DO       IF boolean expression THEN
   statement(s);                     REPEAT
END(* while *);                         statement(s);
                                     UNTIL NOT ( boolean
                                                 expression );
                                  END(* if then *);
```

**Figure 1.76** Relation between WHILE and REPEAT loops

## LOOP

The most general iteration structure is the LOOP. The construction of a LOOP is shown in Figure 1.77.

```
LOOP
   statement(s);
END(* loop *);
```

**Figure 1.77** LOOP

A loop is terminated using an EXIT statement. Figure 1.78 shows the typical construction of a LOOP with an EXIT statement.

```
LOOP
   statement(s);
   IF boolean expression
   THEN
     EXIT;
   END(* if then *);
   statement(s);
END(* loop *);
```

**Figure 1.78** Typical construction of a LOOP

The EXIT statement transfers control to the statement directly below the END statement of the LOOP. The EXIT statement may only be used in connection with LOOPs.

The LOOP structure is a middle-ending loop compared to the top-ending WHILE structure and the bottom-ending REPEAT structure.

Figure 1.79 illustrates a LOOP structure.

```
i := 1;
LOOP
  INC( i );
  writecard( i, 1 );
  IF i = 100
  THEN
    EXIT;
  END(* if then *);
  INC( i, 5 );
END(* loop *);
```

**Figure 1.79** Illustration of LOOP

## FOR Loop

A FOR loop is constructed as shown in Figure 1.80.

```
FOR indexvariable := lowerlimitexpression TO
                        upperlimitexpression DO
  statement(s);
END(* for loop *);
```

**Figure 1.80** FOR loop

The index variable must be declared to be a discrete type such as an integer, cardinal, character, Boolean, or enumeration type. Real variables can never be used as the index in a FOR loop.

The lowerlimit expression and upperlimit expression may be either constants or expressions. The value of the index variable or limits must not be changed within the loop.

If the lower limit is greater than the upper limit, the loop is bypassed and control goes to the line directly below the FOR loop.

Figure 1.81 shows some typical FOR loops.

FOR loops allow an optional increment parameter to be included as follows:

```
FOR index = lowerlimit TO upperlimit BY increment DO
```

where increment may be a constant or expression.

```
VAR
    i : CARDINAL;

FOR i := 1 TO 20 DO
  statement(s);
END(* for loop *);

VAR
    j, z : CARDINAL;

FOR z := i * j + 2 TO i * j + 10 DO
  statement(s);
END(* for loop *);

TYPE color = ( red, blue, green, black, brown, orange );

VAR
   c : color;

FOR c := blue TO brown DO
  statement(s);
END(* for loop *);

VAR
   ch : CHAR;

FOR ch := 'c' TO 'g' DO
  statement(s);
END(* for loop *);
```

**Figure 1.81** Some typical FOR loops

Figure 1.82 shows a code segment that displays the even integers from 1000 down to 0.

```
VAR i : CARDINAL;

FOR i := 1000 TO 0 BY -2 DO
  WriteLn;
  WriteCard( i, 10 );
END(* for loop *);
```

**Figure 1.82** Example of FOR loop

FOR loops are often used when we know, in advance, the number of iterations of the loop. This is, of course, not required since the lower limit and/or upper limit of a FOR loop may be an expression.

FOR loops may be nested. Figure 1.83 illustrates a program segment that computes the 9-column averages and 50-row averages of a matrix (two-dimensional array) with 50 rows and 9 columns of real numbers.

```
CONST
      numbercolumns = 9;
      numberrows    = 50;

TYPE
      colaverage = ARRAY[ 1..numbercolumns ] OF REAL;
      rowaverage = ARRAY[ 1..numberrows ] OF REAL;
      datatype   = ARRAY[ 1..numberrows ],
                        [ 1..numbercolumns ] OF REAL;

VAR
      colav     : colaverage;
      rowav     : rowaverage;
      row, col  : CARDINAL;
      sum       : REAL;

BEGIN

   (* Compute the column averages. *)
   FOR col := 1 TO numbercolumns DO
     sum := 0.0;
     FOR row := 1 TO numberrows DO
       sum := sum + data[ row, col ];
     END(* for loop *);
     colav[ col ] := sum / FLOAT( numberrows );
   END(* for loop *);

   (* Compute the row averages.     *)
   FOR row := 1 TO numberrows DO
     sum := 0.0;
     FOR col := 1 TO numbercolumns DO
       sum := sum + data[ row, col ];
     END(* for loop *);
     rowav[ row ] := sum / FLOAT( numbercolumns );
   END(* for loop *);
```

**Figure 1.83**  Computing row and column averages with nested FOR loops

## Software Engineering:

Figure 1.84 shows the relationship of a FOR loop to a WHILE loop.

```
FOR index := lower TO higher BY increment DO
  statement(s);
END(* for loop *);


index := lower;
WHILE index <= higher DO
  statement(s);
  INC( index, increment );
END(* while loop *);
```

**Figure 1.84**  Relations of FOR loop to WHILE loop

# Procedures and Procedure Functions

A procedure is a logical unit within a module that appears to be a miniature program because it can contain all of the ingredients of a full program. These ingredients include constant, type, and variable declarations; other nested procedures; and a main block of executable code. Indeed, the only distinguishing feature of a procedure compared to a full program module is the possible presence of parameters.

Procedure parameters are used to pass information in and out of the block of code that comprises the procedure.

Procedures are used to isolate the code associated with a specific task.

Procedures can be nested within other procedures to any level, they can call each other within the same scope, and they can call themselves. This last capability is called recursion. (See Recursion.)

## *Software Engineering: Functional Abstraction*

Procedures effectively extend the commands in the language because complex tasks may be accomplished using one identifier in a procedure invocation. Procedures provide the software developer the ability to perform functional abstraction.

The phrase *functional abstraction* suggests a unit of code, a procedure, that performs a specialized function. The decomposition of a problem into functional abstractions is an important design methodology. (See Data Abstraction and Opaque Types.)

## Procedure Parameters and Binding Modes

The syntax for a procedure declaration with parameters is shown in Figure 1.85.

```
PROCEDURE identifier
          (     parameter1 : typeidentifier;
                parameter2 : typeidentifier;
                . . .
            VAR parameter3 : typeidentifier;
                . . .
                                           ):
```

**Figure 1.85** PROCEDURE declaration with parameters

Figure 1.86 shows a typical procedure declaration.

```
PROCEDURE intersection
          ( VAR chset3   : charset          (* out *);
                chset1   : charset          (* in  *);
                chset2   : charset          (* in  *) );
```

**Figure 1.86** Procedure declaration

There are two basic types of procedure parameters, value parameters and reference parameters. Value parameters and reference parameters are used to affect three types of information transfer, called binding modes. These are input only (in), input/output (in/out) and output only (out).

√    When a procedure with parameters is invoked, information that is global to the subprogram is "bound" to the parameters that are declared in the procedure declaration.

## Binding Mode In

A parameter of binding mode *in* allows information contained in a constant, variable, or expression outside of a procedure to be transferred into a procedure. This information may be used by the procedure and changed by the procedure without affecting the value sent into the procedure. Indeed, the value sent into the procedure is decoupled from the value within the procedure.

## Binding Mode In Out

A parameter of binding mode *in/out* allows information contained in a variable global to a procedure to be transferred into a procedure and modified in the procedure. The modification affects the value sent into the procedure. In fact, the value sent in gets changed to the new value established within the procedure.

## Binding Mode Out

A parameter of binding mode *out* transfers information out of a procedure to a variable global to the procedure. The initial value of the output variable is irrelevant.

## Reference and Value Parameters

A reference parameter is distinguished from a value parameter by the presence of a VAR in front of the parameter.

A reference parameter must be bound to a variable (not an expression or a constant) outside of the procedure. The parameter becomes a new name for such a variable. Any changes made to such a parameter within the procedure affect the variable that the parameter is bound to outside of the procedure. The term *reference parameter* is derived from the observation that the parameter shares the same memory location or reference as the outside variable it is bound to.

## Differences Between Value and Reference Parameters

The key differences between value parameters and reference parameters are: copies of information are made for value parameters and not for reference parameters, and value parameters may be bound to constants or expressions, whereas reference parameters must be bound only to outside variables.

In Figure 1.86, reference parameter chset3 is the output set resulting from the intersection of the sets given by value parameters chset1 and chset2.

Figure 1.87 illustrates value and reference parameters and the use of binding modes.

## *Hazard:*

Structured types, such as arrays, may be declared as formal parameters in a procedure. Anonymous array declarations cannot be used as array parameters. The following procedure declaration is illegal because it uses an anonymous type declaration for an array:

```
PROCEDURE illegal
  ( vector : ARRAY[ 1..5 ] OF INTEGER );
```

The proper declaration would be:

```
TYPE intarray = ARRAY[ 1..5 ] OF INTEGER;

PROCEDURE legal
  ( vector : intarray (* in *) );
```

*(continued)*

```
MODULE nameinfo;

  FROM InOut IMPORT
    (* proc *) WriteLn, WriteString, ReadString, ReadCard,
               WriteCard;

  TYPE
      name        = ARRAY[ 0..19 ] OF CHAR;
      phonenumber = ARRAY[ 0..9 ] OF CHAR;


  PROCEDURE getinfo
            ( VAR s     : name          (* out *);
              VAR age   : CARDINAL       (* out *);
              VAR phone : phonenumber (* out *) );

  BEGIN
    WriteString( "Enter your name: " );
    ReadString( s );
    WriteLn; WriteLn;
    WriteString( "Enter your age: " );
    ReadCard( age );
    WriteLn; WriteLn;
    WriteString( "Enter your phone: " );
    ReadString( phone );
  END getinfo;


  PROCEDURE displayinfo
            (     s     : name          (* in *);
                  age   : CARDINAL       (* in *);
                  phone : phonenumber (* in *) );

  BEGIN
    WriteString( "Name   --> " );
    WriteString( s );
    WriteLn; WriteLn;
    WriteString( "Age    --> " );
    WriteCard( age, 1 );
    WriteLn; WriteLn;
    WriteString( "Phone --> " );
    WriteString( phone );
  END displayinfo;


  VAR
      myname  : name;
      myage   : CARDINAL;
      myphone : phonenumber;

BEGIN
  getinfo( myname, myage, myphone );
  displayinfo( myname, myage, myphone );
END nameinfo.
```

**Figure 1.87** Example of value and reference parameters

## *Software Engineering:*

Suppose intarray and procedure legal were declared as follows:

```
TYPE intarray = ARRAY[ 1..8000 ] OF REAL;

PROCEDURE legal
  ( vector : intarray ( * in * ) );
```

When procedure legal is invoked, a copy of an array of 8000 floating-point numbers is made, requiring 64,000 bytes if each real requires 8 bytes. This copy is of little value since the array parameter, vector, is an input parameter. There is no need to decouple the array parameter vector from the array variable sent in. This costs 64,000 bytes.

The solution is to declare vector as a reference parameter as follows:

```
PROCEDURE legal
  ( VAR vector : intarray ( * in * ) );
```

It may appear strange to associate a reference parameter with the binding mode *in*, but this saves a dynamic allocation of 64,000 bytes each time procedure legal is called.

## Open Array Parameters

An open array parameter may be used only as a procedure parameter. Its construction is the following:

```
PROCEDURE identifier
  ( parametername : ARRAY OF basetype );
```

The parametername is bound to an actual one-dimensional array of the base type, but the index range of the one-dimensional array is unknown.

A procedure declaration for computing the length of a string might be given as:

```
PROCEDURE length
  ( str : ARRAY OF CHAR ) : CARDINAL;
```

This procedure would compute the length of an arbitrary-length string.

Using the predefined function HIGH, the one-dimensional array maps to the range

```
0..HIGH( parametername ).
```

For example, if the actual one-dimensional array has the range $-5..3$, the open array parameter has the range $0..8$.

Modula-2 allows only one-dimensional open arrays.

## *Style:*

The following format conventions have been adopted for procedure declarations.

1.  Procedure name on a separate line.

2.  Each parameter on a separate line.

3.  Space for a VAR provided regardless of whether a VAR is present or not.

4.  A comment indicating the binding mode of a parameter provided after the parameter type is given.

5.  The colons line up. The binding modes line up.

## Procedure Functions

There are two types of procedures, pure procedures (henceforth called *procedures*) and procedure functions. The former cannot be used in expressions, whereas the latter must be used in expressions. Procedure functions return a value.

We must emphasize that it is illegal to use procedures in an expression, only procedure functions. Thus the intended use of a procedure should dictate whether it is declared as a procedure or procedure function.

## *Hazard:*

Some implementations of Modula-2 impose restrictions on the type of data that can be returned by a procedure function. Specifically, some implementations do not allow a structured data type such as an array to be returned by a procedure function. The Modula-2 language definition imposes no such restriction. You should consult your Modula-2 implementation guide to determine whether your implementation allows functions to return structured data.

Figure 1.88 shows a typical procedure function.

```
PROCEDURE strlessthan;
        (     str1, str2 : string (* in *) ) : BOOLEAN;
```

**Figure 1.88** Typical procedure function

## Scope and Visibility

Local variables are those variables defined within a procedure.

Memory allocation for local variables and value parameters occurs when a procedure is invoked, and memory deallocation occurs when a procedure is exited. The run-time environment provided by the operating system manages the allocation and deallocation of memory space for local variables and value parameters.

## *Hazard:*

Because of the dynamic nature of the memory allocation for local variables within a procedure, it is possible for a program to run out of memory while the program is executing. This may occur if a procedure with memory-intensive local variables or value parameters is invoked. Some compilers may impose a limit on local variable declarations so that such run-time memory crashes do not occur.

## Scope

A local variable's scope extends from its point of declaration down to the end of the procedure in which it is declared.

## Overloading of Variable Names

If the name for a local variable within a procedure duplicates the name of a global variable, only the local variable is visible within the procedure. Such overloading of variable names may be used by a programmer to mask a variable global to a procedure.

Figure 1.89 illustrates local variable name overloading.

```
(* Main program *)
VAR
    a, b, c : CARDINAL;

  PROCEDURE overload
            (    a : CHAR );

  VAR
      b : REAL;

  BEGIN
    Write( a ); (* See section 3, output.  'A' is output. *)
    b := 6.5;
    WriteReal( b, 20 ); (* Output 6.5 *)
    c := 2;
  END overload;

BEGIN (* Main program *)
  a := 3;
  b := 4;
  overload( 'A' );
  WriteCard( a, 5 ); (* Output 3 *)
  WriteCard( b, 5 ); (* Output 4 *)
  WriteCard( c, 5 ); (* Output 2 *)
  ...
```

**Figure 1.89** Local variable name overloading

When procedure overload is invoked, two variables b exist, the local real variable b in procedure overload and the global variable b in the main program. The assignment of 6.5 to local variable b does not change the value of the global variable b that is 4.

In procedure overload, parameter a and local variable b mask their global counterparts.

The scope of local real variable b extends from the beginning of procedure overload to the end statement of this procedure. The range of visibility for global cardinal variable b extends from the beginning of the main program to the end of the main program. The scope of this global variable covers the entire program except where it is overloaded.

## RETURN Statement

The RETURN statement is used to exit a procedure or procedure function. When RETURN is invoked in a procedure or procedure function, an immediate exit from the procedure occurs.

In a procedure function, the RETURN statement must be followed by a constant or expression of the same type as given in the procedure function declaration. This provides the value returned by the procedure function.

Figure 1.90 shows a typical use of RETURN in a procedure and procedure function.

```
PROCEDURE procedurename;

BEGIN
  statement(s);
  IF boolean expression
  THEN
    RETURN;
  END(* if then *);
  statement(s);
END procedurename;

PROCEDURE functionname() : typeidentifier;

VAR ...
    v : typeidentifier;

BEGIN
  statement(s);
  RETURN v;
END functionname;
```

**Figure 1.90** Typical use of RETURN in a procedure and procedure function

## Procedure Types

In Modula-2, procedures may be designated as types. This provides a clean mechanism whereby procedures may be passed as parameters to other procedures. Variables may be declared in terms of procedure types.

A procedure type declaration establishes a template for a whole class of procedure variables or formal procedure parameters. The compiler verifies that a member of this class (an actual procedure or procedure function) contains the same sequence and type of parameters, and in the case of a procedure function, returns the same type as the template.

The syntax of a procedure type is given as:

```
TYPE
  ident = PROCEDURE( type1, type2, ..., typek );
```

Figure 1.91 shows some procedure type and variable declarations and the use of procedure types as formal procedure parameters.

```
TYPE

    tree = POINTER TO node;

    node = RECORD
             info  : CARDINAL;
             left  : tree;
             right : tree;
           END(* record *);

    twovarrealtype = PROCEDURE( REAL, REAL ) : REAL;

    realtype       = PROCEDURE( REAL ) : REAL;

    displaytype    = PROCEDURE( tree );


    PROCEDURE display
             (     t : tree );

    BEGIN
      IF t # NIL
      THEN
        WriteCard( t^.info, 10 );
        display( t^.left );
        display( t^.right );
      END(* if then *);
    END display;


    PROCEDURE f
             (     x : REAL (* in *) ) : REAL;

    BEGIN
      RETURN 3.6 * x * x - 2.4 * x + 1.2;
    END f;


    PROCEDURE g
             (     x, y : REAL (* in *) ) : REAL;

    BEGIN
      RETURN 2.4 * x * y - 1.4 * x + 2.6 * y + 34.5;
    END g;


    PROCEDURE displayprocedure
             (     t : tree        (* in *);
                   d : displaytype (* in *) );

    BEGIN
      statement(s);
    END displayprocedure;
```

```
VAR
      value1    : realtype;
      value2    : twovarrealtype;
      r         : REAL;
      x, y      : REAL;
      rootnode  : tree;

BEGIN
   ...

      (* We pass procedure display into procedure
         displayprocedure as a parameter.                    *)
      (* Assume that rootnode has been assigned a value.     *)
      displayprocedure( rootnode, display );
      (* Assume that variables r, x, and y have previously been
         assigned values.                                    *)
      value1 := f;
      r := r - value1( x );
      value1 := sin; (* sin is imported from external module
                        Math0.                               *)
      r := r + value1( 3.0 * x );
      value1 := tan; (* tan is imported from external module
                        Math0.                               *)
      r := value1( 4.0 + 2.0 / x );
      value2 := g;
      r := r + value2( x, 2.0 * y );
   ...
```

**Figure 1.91** The declaration of procedure types and variables

## *Software Engineering:*

Procedure types may be exploited in writing general purpose generic software. For example, suppose a procedure integrate is developed for numerically integrating a real function of one real variable (realtype in Figure 1.91) over definite limits. Such a procedure must work for any integrand function of type realtype. Figure 1.92 shows the interface to such a numerical integration procedure and typical calls to procedure integrate.

## *Comment:*

The real argument, x, in procedure function f(x) must be supplied within procedure integrate. Only the function f is passed into procedure integrate.

As another practical illustration of procedure parameters, a generic tree insertion procedure is shown in Figure 1.93.

Here, elementtype is defined as a transparent type in an external module elements and imported into the module containing procedure insertion. (See Library Modules.)

```
(* Assume the same type and variable declarations as in
   Figure 1.91.                                          *)

PROCEDURE integrate
          (  integrand  : realtype (* in *);
             lowerlimit :  REAL     (* in *);
             upperlimit :  REAL     (* in *) ) : REAL;

BEGIN
  (* Body of integrate procedure.                        *)
END integrate;


BEGIN
  ...
  value1 := f;
  r := integrate( value1, 14.6, 17.9 );
  value1 := cos; (* Imported from Math0 *)
  r := integrate( value1, -3.6, 1.2 );
  ...
```

**Figure 1.92** Interface and call to numerical integration procedure

```
TYPE

      tree = POINTER TO node;

      node = RECORD
               info  : CARDINAL;
               left  : tree;
               right : tree;
             END(* record *);

TYPE equaltype      = PROCEDURE( elementtype, elementtype ) :
                        BOOLEAN;

TYPE lessthantype   = PROCEDURE( elementtype, elementtype ) :
                        BOOLEAN;


PROCEDURE insertion
          ( VAR t          : tree           (* in/out *);
                item        : elementtype    (* in     *);
                equal       : equaltype      (* in     *);
                lessthan    : lessthantype   (* in     *) );
(* Inserts the elementtype item into tree t.              *)

  VAR
     found   : BOOLEAN;
     parent  : tree;
     current : tree;

  BEGIN
    found := FALSE;
    parent := NIL;
    current := t;
    WHILE ( current # NIL ) AND ( NOT found ) DO
      IF equal( current^.info, item )
      THEN
        found := TRUE;
```

```
    ELSE
      parent := current;
      IF lessthan( item, current^.info )
      THEN
        current := current^.left;
      ELSE
        current := current^.right;
      END(* if then  *);
    END(* if then  *);
  END(* while loop *);
  IF NOT found
  THEN
    IF parent = NIL
    THEN
      t := makenode( item );
    ELSE
      IF lessthan( item , parent^.info )
      THEN
        addleft( parent, item );
      ELSE
        addright( parent, item );
      END(* if then *);
    END(* if then *);
  END(* if then *);
END insert;
```

**Figure 1.93** A generic tree insertion procedure

In order to insert an item into a tree, it is necessary that facilities for comparing the item being inserted with an item already stored in a tree node be available to procedure insertion. If procedure insertion is to qualify as a generic insertion procedure, then elementtype is not known at the time procedure insertion is compiled. Formal procedure parameters equal and lessthan represent procedures created by the programmer and passed to the generic insertion procedure after the programmer defines elementtype. The values of elementtype that are used by procedure parameters equal and lessthan must be supplied by procedure insertion. See *Data Structures Using Modula-2* by Sincovec and Wiener, Wiley, 1986.

Figure 1.94 shows two typical procedures, equal and lessthan, that may be sent into procedure insertion if elementtype is defined as type CARDINAL.

## *Hazard:*

It is essential that the sequence and type of parameter(s) that are defined for a particular procedure exactly match those of the procedure type used in a formal parameter list. For example, if proceduretype is defined as

```
TYPE proceduretype = PROCEDURE( VAR REAL );
```

*(continued)*

```
PROCEDURE equal
          ( item1, item2 : elementtype          (* in *) ) :
BOOLEAN;

BEGIN
  RETURN item1.age = item2.age;
END equal;


PROCEDURE lessthan
          ( item1, item2 : elementtype          (* in *) ) :
BOOLEAN;

BEGIN
  RETURN item1.age < item2.age;
END lessthan;
```

**Figure 1.94** Two typical procedures equal and lessthan

and a procedure, example, is defined as

```
PROCEDURE example
  ( r : REAL );

BEGIN
  statement(s);
END example;
```

then an attempt to pass procedure example to another procedure such as

```
PROCEDURE generic( f : proceduretype );
```

will fail at compile time. The compiler will detect a mismatch between the value parameter r in procedure example and the required reference parameter of type real required in f as a proceduretype.

## Recursion

A recursive control structure is a generalization of an iterative control structure. It is not necessary, as with iteration, that each recursive call be completed before the next one is started.

Recursive control is established in Modula-2 by having a procedure call itself or a procedure function call itself. It is the programmer's responsibility to ensure that infinite loops do not exist at the procedure call level.

Before a recursive call is begun and program flow interrupted, all value parameters and local variables that are in effect just before the recursive procedure invocation are saved on the system stack. When the recursive call is completed and control returns to the procedure one line below the recursive call, all the value parameters and local variables that were previously pushed onto the stack are popped from the stack.

## *Hazard:*

A stack overflow condition can occur if one or more local variables or value parameters require a great deal of storage and many recursive calls are made.

Figure 1.95 shows an example of a recursive procedure for performing a binary search on an ordered array of numbers.

```
CONST
     size = 2000;

TYPE
     vectortype = ARRAY[ 1..size ] OF CARDINAL;

VAR
     pos : CARDINAL;

PROCEDURE binarysrch
          (    low    : CARDINAL    (* in *);
               high   : CARDINAL    (* in *);
               key    : CARDINAL    (* in *);
               vector : vectortype (* in *) );
(* The value of pos is found.                        *)

VAR
     middle : CARDINAL;

BEGIN
  IF low <= high
  THEN
    middle := ( low + high ) DIV 2;
    IF key = vector[ middle ]
    THEN
      pos := middle;
    ELSIF key < vector[ middle ]
    THEN
      binarysrch( low, middle, key, vector );
    ELSE
      binarysrch( middle + 1, high, key, vector );
    END(* if then *);
  END(* if then *);
END search;
```

**Figure 1.95** Binary search procedure using recursion

## Internal Modules

An internal module is a logical unit nested within another module or procedure that is used to create an isolated environment for controlling the scope and visibility of identifiers.

Information is passed into and out of internal modules with IMPORT and EXPORT lists. These lists act as input and output conduits that penetrate through the opaque membrane of the module.

In order for entities such as constants, types, variables or procedures to be visible inside an internal module they must be explicitly imported. In order for such entities to be visible outside of an internal module they must be explicitly exported.

Figure 1.96 shows the declaration of an internal module and typical import and export lists.

```
MODULE mainprogram;

  FROM InOut IMPORT
    (* proc *) WriteLn, WriteString, WriteCard;

  MODULE internal;

    IMPORT
      (* proc *) WriteLn; WriteString;
      (* Brings these two procedures within scope.       *)

    EXPORT
      (* proc *) internalproc1, internalproc2;
      (* Makes these two procedures visible outside of the
         scope of module internal.                       *)

    PROCEDURE internalproc1;
    BEGIN
      WriteLn;
      WriteString( "Inside internal procedure 1." );
    END internalproc1;

    PROCEDURE internalproc2;
    BEGIN
      WriteLn;
      WriteString( "Inside internal procedure 2." );
    END internalproc2;

  END internal;


  BEGIN
    (* These two procedures are visible in the main program
       because they appear on the export list of internal
       module internal.                                  *)
    internalproc1;
    internalproc2;
  END mainprogram.
```

**Figure 1.96** The declaration of an internal module

The presence of WriteLn and WriteString in the scope surrounding module internal does not make these procedures visible inside module internal. Only the IMPORT list achieves this.

## Initialization Code

An internal module may contain an optional block of code called initialization code contained within a begin and the end statement of the module. This initialization code is executed exactly once when the internal module is activated. Such activation occurs when the logical unit enclosing the internal module becomes activated. Such an enclosing logical unit may be another internal module, a procedure, or a main program module.

If several internal modules are declared within a logical unit, the initialization code is executed in the order that the internal modules are declared in the logical unit.

Figure 1.97 shows the placement of initialization code in internal modules.

```
MODULE internal;

   IMPORT list;

   EXPORT list;

   Internal declarations;

BEGIN
   (* Initialization code *)
END internal;
```

**Figure 1.97** Placement of initialization code in an internal module

## *Software Engineering:*

An important and major use for an internal module is hiding one or more variables while keeping their value alive. Global variables stay alive for the full duration of a program but are visible everywhere in the program except in isolated sections where they may be masked. This global visibility may be a liability inasmuch as any procedure in the program may change and corrupt the value of the global variable.

Figure 1.98 illustrates how an internal module may be used to hide several variables but keep them alive.

```
MODULE illustration;

  FROM InOut IMPORT
     (* proc *) WriteLn, WriteString, WriteCard;

VAR
     a, b : REAL;

  MODULE hide;
  (* This internal module hides the value of variables
     a, b, and c but keeps them alive.                    *)

    IMPORT
      (* proc *) WriteLn, WriteString, WriteCard;

    EXPORT
      (* proc *) display;

    VAR
       a, b, c : CARDINAL;


    PROCEDURE display;

    BEGIN
       WriteLn;
       WriteString( "The values of the data = " );
       WriteCard( a, 5 );
       WriteCard( b, 5 );
       WriteCard( c, 5 );
    END display;

  BEGIN
     a := 14;
     b :- 12;
     c := 10;
  END hide;

BEGIN(* Main program *)
  a := 21.6;
  b := -11.8;
  display;
END illustration.
```

**Figure 1.98** Internal module used to hide variables

## Library Modules

Modula-2 supports three types of compilation units (blocks of code that may be separately compiled): definition modules, implementation modules, and program modules. Definition and implementation modules are called library modules. They are generally written to encapsulate reusable software components: a data abstraction and a set of functional abstractions. (See Data Abstraction and Opaque Types.)

Entities such as constants, types, variables and procedures that are exported from a definition module may be used (imported) in many client modules. In a recent change to the Modula-2 language specification, all entities declared in a definition module are automatically visible outside of this module when brought into scope by an appropriate IMPORT list in a client module. Prior to this language change, an EXPORT list was required to make entities available to client modules. Many existing compilers have not yet implemented this latest language change and still require EXPORT lists.

Every definition module is required to have an associated implementation module. This module contains the implementation details of the data types and procedures defined in the definition module.

A definition module may be compared to a socket. It represents an interface, a promise of software components. Only procedure declarations (stubs) are allowed in a definition module. Like a socket, one may plug into a definition module. The implementation module contains the software circuitry, the wiring behind the socket. It fulfills the promises made in the definition module. In addition to repeating procedure declarations exactly as they appear in the definition module, full procedure bodies (implementation details) must be provided in the implementation module.

## Separate vs. Independent Compilation

A Modula-2 software system consists of an interrelated set of library modules and a main driver program module. IMPORT lists provide the linkage between entities defined and promised in definition modules and client modules, where the entities can be accessed and used.

When a reference is made in a client module to an entity that is imported from a library module, the compiler enforces strong type checking and verifies that the entity is used properly in the client module. Indeed, the compiler treats imported entities as if they had been declared in the client module.

The strong type checking across compilation boundaries is an important and extremely useful feature of Modula-2. This feature is called separate compilation. This is in contrast to independent compilation in which references may be made to entities in external modules with no type checking performed to ensure that the references are legal. FORTRAN and C are languages that use independent compilation.

## Order of Compilation

Because of the dependencies among modules in a Modula-2 software system, exporting modules (definition modules) must be compiled before client modules that import one or more entities from these exporting modules. If a change is made to an exporting module and such a module is recompiled, all client modules in the system must be recompiled. Figure 1.99 lists some legal and illegal sequences of compilation for a small Modula-2 software system.

```
Module Name          Entities Imported      Entities Exported
----------           -----------------      -----------------

definition m1        none                   a1, b1, c1, d1

implementation m1    FROM m2:               none
                       a2, b2

definition m2        FROM m1:               a2, b2
                       a1

implementation m2    FROM m1:               none
                       c1, d1

                     FROM m3:
                       b3, c3

definition m3        none                   a3, b3, c3

implementation m3    none                   none


              Some legal compilation sequences
              --------------------------------

1.   def m1
2.   def m2
3.   def m3
4.   implementation modules in any order

1.   def m3
2.   def m1
3    def m2
4.   implementation modules in any order
```

```
1.  def m1
2.  def m2
3.  imp m1
4.  def m3
5.  remaining implementation modules in any order

          Some illegal compilation sequences
          ----------------------------------

1.  def m2 (def m2 is a client of m1; must be compiled
           after def m1)
2.  def m1
3.  def m3
4.  implementation modules in any order

1.  def m1
2.  imp m1 (imp m1 is a client of m2; must be compiled after
           def m2)
3.  def m2
4.  imp m2 (imp m2 is a client of m3; must be compiled after
           def m3)
5.  def m3
6.  remaining implementation modules
```

**Figure 1.99** Some legal and illegal sequences of compilation

## Version Control

Modula-2 systems are equipped with version control systems. The details of these systems may vary from vendor to vendor. The basic idea may be described as follows.

When a definition module is compiled, a time stamp is embossed in the symbol file (object file) produced by the compiler. The object code of the implementation module acquires the same time stamp as the definition module. Every client module acquires the time stamp of the definition module.

At link time, the version control system verifies that the time stamps in all definition modules match the time stamps in their client modules. Any mismatch is indicated by the version control system.

If a definition module is recompiled (even without being modified), a new time stamp is created and cmbcddcd in the definition module's object file. If all client modules are not recompiled, the mismatch of time stamps is flagged and indicated to the programmer at link time. No code is generated.

## *Software Engineering:*

A major problem in the past has been the high-level integration of software components developed by several programmers working on a team. These problems develop when outdated modules are accidentally used by one or more team members. The version control system required of Modula-2 systems will more than likely avoid such costly software integration problems.

## *Hazard:*

Definition modules should not be changed and recompiled without good reason. In a large software system with many interrelated modules, a significant recompilation overhead may result from recompiling one or more key definition modules. (See Data Abstraction and Opaque Types.)

## Definition Modules

The interface to a set of software components is specified in a definition module. As indicated before, a definition module is a software socket. The resources specified in such a module may be tapped by any client module.

A definition module may contain constants, types, variables, and procedure stubs for export to other modules. There is no body of code associated with a definition module. Clear documentation should be provided with each procedure stub to facilitate ease of use.

Figure 1.100 shows the interface to a character set package.

## *Software Engineering:*

The documentation that usually accompanies a software library should be embedded as comments in a definition module. This module serves as an interface to a programmer. Without clear comments, such an interface is of little value. Figure 1.100 contains an example of software documentation embedded in a definition module.

```
DEFINITION MODULE charsets;
(* This module defines the character set data type.        *)

   EXPORT QUALIFIED (* Export list no longer required *)
      (* const *) nullset, uppercase, lowercase, numeral,
      (* type *) charset,
      (* proc *) include, exclude, inset, union, intersection;
```

*(continued)*

```
CONST
      piecesize    = 16;  (* TSIZE bitset. *)
      setsize      = 128; (* size of universe set. *)
      pieces       = setsize DIV piecesize;
      maxpiece     = pieces - 1;


TYPE
      piecerange   = [  0 .. maxpiece  ];
      charset      = ARRAY piecerange OF BITSET;


VAR
      nullset      : charset; (* behaves like a constant *)
      uppercase    : charset; (* behaves like a constant *)
      lowercase    : charset; (* behaves like a constant *)
      numeral      : charset; (* behaves like a constant *)


PROCEDURE include
          ( VAR chset    : charset            (* in/out *);
                ch       : CHAR               (* in     *) );
(*
   Used to add ch to an existing set chset.

   Input Parameters
   ----------------
   ch    - Character to be included in set.

   Output Parameters
   -----------------
   chset - The character set to have ch added to it.
                                                           *)



PROCEDURE exclude
          ( VAR chset    : charset            (* in/out *);
                ch       : CHAR               (* in     *) );
(*
   Used to remove ch from an existing set chset.

   Input Parameters
   ----------------
   ch    - Character to be excluded from set.

   Output Parameters
   -----------------
   chset - The character set to have ch removed from it.
                                                           *)



PROCEDURE inset
          (     chset    : charset            (* in    *);
                ch       : CHAR               (* in    *) ) :
BOOLEAN;
```

*(continued)*

```
(*
    Returns true if ch is in chset, otherwise returns
    false.

    Input Parameters
    ----------------
    chset - The set being tested for the presence of ch.
    ch    - If ch is present in chset, the procedure
            returns true, otherwise false.
                                                        *)
PROCEDURE union
        ( VAR chset3          : charset  (* out  *);
              chset1, chset2  : charset  (* in   *) );
(*
    Returns the union of sets chset1  and chset2.

    Input Parameters
    ----------------
    chset1, chset2 - The two sets that we wish to form the
                     union of.

    Output Parameters
    ----------------
    chset3         - The union of sets chset1 and chset2.
                                                        *)
PROCEDURE intersection
        ( VAR chset3  : charset          (* out  *);
              chset1  : charset          (* in   *);
              chset2  : charset          (* in   *) );
(*
    Returns the intersection of sets chset1 and chset2.

    Input Parameters
    ----------------
    chset1, chset2 - The two sets that we wish to form the
                     intersection of.

    Output Parameters
    ----------------
    chset3         - The intersection of sets chset1 and
                     chset2.
                                                        *)

END charsets.
```

**Figure 1.100**  Definition module of character sets

## Opaque Types

An opaque type may be declared only in a definition module. Such a declaration uses the reserved word TYPE followed by a type identifier. Some examples are:

```
TYPE tree;
```

TYPE stack;

The representational details (data structure) of an opaque type are given in the implementation module. The internal structure of an opaque type given in the implementation module is inaccessible to any client module. This is called data hiding. The use of data hiding with opaque types plays a major role in object-oriented software design. (See Data Abstraction and Opaque Types.)

## Implementation Modules

The promises made in a definition module must be delivered in an implementation module.

All opaque types must be implemented as data structures in such a module. The Modula-2 language specification currently calls for all opaque types to be implemented as pointer or address types. This permits the compiler to allocate memory for one address for every opaque type encountered.

Every procedure stub (interface) given in the definition module must be repeated in the implementation module. A good text editor is useful here. In addition, the body of each procedure must be provided. It is in the implementation module that the usual low-level design decisions about data structures and algorithms are made.

Figure 1.101 shows the implementation module for the character set definition module given in Figure 1.100.

```
IMPLEMENTATION MODULE charsets;

PROCEDURE include
          ( VAR chset     : charset        (* in/out *);
                ch        : CHAR           (* in      *) );
BEGIN
  IF ORD( ch ) < 128
  THEN
  INCL( chset[ ORD( ch ) DIV piecesize ],
        ORD( ch ) MOD
     piecesize );
  END(* if then *);
END include;
```

*(continued)*

```
PROCEDURE exclude
        ( VAR chset      : charset          (* in/out *);
              ch         : CHAR             (* in     *) );

BEGIN
  IF ORD( ch ) < 128
  THEN
    EXCL( chset[ ORD( ch ) DIV piecesize ],  ORD( ch ) MOD
          piecesize );
  END(* if then *);
END exclude;


PROCEDURE inset
        (     chset      : charset          (* in  *);
              ch         : CHAR             (* in  *) ) :
BOOLEAN;

BEGIN
  IF ORD( ch ) < 128
  THEN
    RETURN ORD(  ch  ) MOD piecesize IN chset[ ORD( ch )
    DIV piecesize  ];
  ELSE
    RETURN FALSE;
  END(* if then *);
END inset;


PROCEDURE union
        ( VAR chset3         : charset  (* out  *);
              chset1, chset2 : charset  (* in   *) );

  VAR
      piece              : piecerange;

BEGIN
  FOR piece := 0 TO maxpiece DO
    chset3[  piece  ] := chset1[  piece  ] +
                         chset2[  piece  ];
  END(* for loop *);
END union;


PROCEDURE intersection
        ( VAR chset3    : charset          (* out  *);
              chset1    : charset          (* in   *);
              chset2    : charset          (* in   *) );

  VAR
      piece              : piecerange;

BEGIN
  FOR piece := 0 TO maxpiece DO
    chset3[  piece  ] := chset1[  piece  ] *
                         chset2[  piece  ];
  END(* for loop *);
END intersection;
```

```
VAR
        ch                      : CHAR;
        piece                   : CARDINAL;


BEGIN(* initialization code *)
  FOR piece := 0 TO maxpiece DO
    nullset[ piece ] := {};
  END(* for loop *);
  uppercase := nullset;
  FOR ch := 'A' TO 'Z' DO
    include( uppercase, ch );
  END(* for loop *);
  lowercase := nullset;
  FOR ch := 'a' TO 'z' DO
    include( lowercase, ch );
  END(* for loop *);
  numeral := nullset;
  FOR ch := '0' TO '9' DO
    include( numeral, ch );
  END(* for loop *);
END charsets.
```

**Figure 1.101** Implementation module for character sets

## *Software Engineering:*

It is important to note that if changes are made to either the data structures or algorithms in the implementation module and this module is recompiled, no other modules in the software system need to be changed or recompiled. Typically, these are the types of changes that are made during routine software maintenance. Modula-2's protection against fall-out effects during routine program maintenance makes this language ideally suited for large software development projects involving large teams of programmers.

## Module Initialization Code

Implementation modules, like internal modules, may optionally contain initialization code as the last block of code in the module. Figure 1.101 contains an example of initialization code. This initialization code defines several set variables (nullset, uppercase, lowercase) that act as set constants.

Initialization code is executed exactly once. It is triggered by a client module that includes the library module's name on an import list. If several implementation modules contain initialization code, this code is executed in the order of IMPORT list declaration.

## *Hazard:*

When constructing a large software system in which several implementation modules contain initialization code, the programmer must exercise caution in sequencing the initialization code properly. An incorrect sequence can cause harmful side effects.

## Lifetime of Static Variables

In Modula-2, it is possible to achieve the objective of making a variable stay alive for the duration of a program while controlling its visibility. Any global variable declared in an implementation module remains alive for the full duration of a program. Such a variable is totally invisible and inaccessible outside of the implementation module. Such a variable is a private variable of use only in the implementation module.

Figure 1.102 shows a practical application of alive variables: a segment of an implementation module that contains an excellent random number generator.

```
VAR
    rand2on  : BOOLEAN;
    seed1,
    seed2    : CARDINAL;


PROCEDURE rand2
            ( machineseed     : BOOLEAN   (* in *);
              s1, s2          : CARDINAL  (* in *) ) :
CARDINAL;

    VAR
        c                     : CARDINAL;
        h,
        m,
        s,
        hu                    : CARDINAL;

BEGIN
  IF NOT rand2on
  THEN (* First time procedure rand is called.        *)
    IF machineseed
    THEN (* User wishes the initial seeds to be generated
           from a real-time clock.                    *)
      gettime( h,  m,  s,  hu );
      (* Returns the current hour, minute, second and
         hundreth of a second from a real-time clock.  *)
      seed1 := hu + m;
      seed2 := h * s;
```

```
                          ELSE
                            seed1 := s1;
                            seed2 := s2;
                          END(* if then *);
                          seed1 := 2 * seed1;
                          seed2 := 2 * seed2;
                          IF seed1 > max
                          THEN
                            seed1 := seed1 - max;
                          END(* if then *);
                          IF seed2 > max
                          THEN
                            seed2 := seed2 - max;
                          END(* if then *);
                          rand2on := TRUE;
                        END(* if then *);
                        c := seed1 + seed2;
                        IF c > max
                        THEN
                          c := c - max;
                        END(* if then *);
                        c := 2 * c;
                        IF c > max
                        THEN
                          c := c - max;
                        END(* if then *);
                        seed1 := seed2;
                        seed2 := c;
                        setmode( mode );
                        RETURN c;
                      END rand2;


              PROCEDURE rand
                         (      machineseed : BOOLEAN  (* in *);
                         seed1, seed2 : CARDINAL (* in *) ) : REAL;
    (*
       Returns a random real between 0.00 and 1.00.

       Input Parameters
       ----------------
       machineseed  - If true, the computer generates initial
                      seed using its real time clock. The
                      values of seed1 and seed2 are ignored.
                      If false, the values of seed1 and seed2
                      are used to initialize the random number
                      generator.
       seed1, seed2 - If machine seed is false, used to
                      initialize the random number generator.
                                                              *)

    BEGIN
      RETURN FLOAT( rand2( machineseed, seed1, seed2 ) )
                   / 32767.0;
    END rand;

BEGIN(* Initialization code *)
  rand2on := FALSE;
END utilities.
```

**Figure 1.102** A random number generator using alive variables for the seeds

The alive variables seed1 and seed2 play a central role in the logic of the random number generator. It is essential that seed1 and seed2 retain their values for the duration of a program because the integrity of the sequence of random numbers is critically dependent on seed1 and seed2. These variables are totally hidden and inaccessible (protected) from any outside module.

# Data Abstraction and Opaque Types

For a full discussion of this subject see *Software Engineering With Modula-2 and Ada* by Wiener, Sincovec, Wiley, 1984.

The essence of problem solving is abstraction. Problem solving is central to software development and abstraction plays a major role in software development.

Abstraction may be described as identifying essential concepts while ignoring inessential details. In software development, a problem solver may typically model a system in terms of a set of objects, operations, and processes. Such a model represents an abstraction of a system.

Abstraction is used to help us partition a complex problem into smaller, more manageable subsystems or modules. Each of the resulting subsystems or modules may be further partitioned into still smaller components.

Modules provide a software designer and implementor with the basis for partitioning a software system into physical and logical units, each with a well-defined interface. Modules also allow a programmer to carefully control the visibility of declared entities and to hide them from regions within a software system where they ought to remain inaccessible.

The essential feature of an abstract data type is the separation of its concept and implementation. The term *data hiding* is used to describe this ability. The programmer or user of the data abstraction is given a precise description of the set of values and set of operations that define the abstract data type, but the implementation of the type is hidden and inaccessible.

Data abstraction provides a mechanism to group logically related software components. This leads to cleaner software design, easier testing, and simplified maintenance.

Data hiding (the use of abstract data types) offers a programmer the ability to guarantee the integrity of the values of an abstract data type. The programmer cannot manipulate the internal representation of a data type because this representation is invisible and inaccessible. Consistency of usage is guaranteed because only the operations defined for the abstract data type may be performed by users of the type. This consistency of usage is very important in designing and implementing large multiprogrammer software projects. Many common errors may be avoided because of the enforcement of consistency of usage.

The separation of the definition of an abstract data type from its implementation allows the programmer the option of changing the implementation without any fallout effects on the rest of the software system. Only the interface to the abstract data type, its definition, determines its relationship to the rest of the software system.

Figure 1.103 shows the interface to a dynamic string abstract data type. The interface to the dynamic string given by the 15 procedure stubs provides the functional abstractions (operations) that are possible on this abstract data type. Consistency of usage is guaranteed because only the defined operations may be performed on the string abstract data type.

```
DEFINITION MODULE dynamicstring;
(* Encapsulates a dynamic string abstract data type. The
   implementation details are given in DATA STRUCTURES USING
   MODULA-2 by Sincovec and Wiener, Wiley, 1986.           *)

   EXPORT QUALIFIED
     (* type *)   string,
     (* proc *)   define, createnull, copy, concatenate,
                  search, delete, insert, extract, length,
                  equal, lessthan, readstring, writestring,
                  convertarray, convertliteral;

   TYPE string;
   (* Abstract data type.                                  *)

   PROCEDURE define
             ( VAR str        : string       (* out     *) );
   (* This procedure must be used before any other procedures
      on str.                                               *)


   PROCEDURE createnull
             ( VAR str        : string       (* in/out *) );
   (* A defined string, str, is set to blank.              *)


   PROCEDURE copy
             (     str1       : string       (* in     *) );
                 VAR str2     : string       (* in/out *) );
   (* Defined string, str1, is copied into defined string
      str2.                                                *)
```

*(continued)*

```
PROCEDURE concatenate
        (       str1            : string         (* in    *);
                str2            : string         (* in    *);
                VAR result      : string         (* in/out *) );
(* Defined string str2 is concatenated to defined string
    str1 to produce defined string result.                 *)


PROCEDURE search
        (       str             : string         (* in    *);
                pattern         : string         (* in    *);
                start           : CARDINAL        (* in    *);
                VAR location    : CARDINAL        (* out   *) );
(* The location of defined string pattern is output if
    pattern is present in defined string str.  If pattern
    is not present, the location zero is returned.         *)


PROCEDURE delete
        ( VAR str               : string         (* in/out *);
                start           : CARDINAL        (* in    *);
                count           : CARDINAL        (* in    *) );
(* For defined string str, count characters are deleted
    starting at start.  If count is too large, nothing is
    deleted.                                               *)


PROCEDURE insert
        ( VAR str               : string         (* in/out *);
                substr          : string         (* in    *);
                start           : CARDINAL        (* in    *) );

(* For defined string str, the defined substring substr is
    inserted into str beginning at position start.         *)


PROCEDURE extract
        (       str             : string         (* in    *);
                start           : CARDINAL        (* in    *);
                count           : CARDINAL        (* in    *);
                VAR substr      : string         (* in/out *) );
(* For defined string str, count characters beginning at
    start are deposited into defined string substr.        *)


PROCEDURE length
        (       str             : string         (* in    *) ) :
CARDINAL;
(* The size of defined string str is returned.             *)


PROCEDURE equal
        (       str1            : string         (* in    *);
                str2            : string         (* in    *) ) :
BOOLEAN;
(* If defined strings str1 and str2 are equal, true is
    returned otherwise false is returned.                  *)


PROCEDURE lessthan
        (       str1            : string         (* in    *);
                str2            : string         (* in    *) ) :
```

```
                BOOLEAN;
                (* If defined str1 is alphabetically smaller than defined
                    string str2, true is returned otherwise false.        *)


                PROCEDURE readstring
                         ( VAR str         : string         (* in/out *) );
                (* Defined string str is assigned a value from keyboard
                    using 'RETURN' as a terminator.                        *)


                PROCEDURE writestring
                         ( str           : string         (* in      *) );
                (* Defined string str is written to terminal.             *)


                PROCEDURE convertarray
                         (       chars     : ARRAY OF CHAR (* in      *);
                                 count     : CARDINAL      (* in      *);
                             VAR str       : string        (* in/out *) );
                (* An ordinary static "string", chars, of size count, is
                    converted to a defined dynamic string str.             *)


                PROCEDURE convertliteral
                         (       chars     : ARRAY OF CHAR (* in      *);
                             VAR str       : string        (* in/out *) );
                (* A literal, chars, is converted to a defined dynamic
                    string str.                                            *)

                END dynamicstring.
```

**Figure 1.103**  Interface to dynamic string abstract data type

# Low-Level Features: Bit and Byte Manipulations

Modula-2 provides low-level facilities for manipulating bits and bytes. The low-level functionality of C is available in Modula-2.

Extreme caution must be exercised in programming at a low level. Portability is almost always at risk. Even small changes in hardware may render low-level code null and void. The advantage of low-level coding is primarily run-time efficiency—speed.

## Module SYSTEM

Standard library module SYSTEM, available on all Modula-2 implementations, contains the support for low-level operations. Figure 1.104 shows the software resources available in module SYSTEM.

```
TYPE byte;

TYPE WORD;

TYPE ADDRESS;

TYPE PROCESS;

PROCEDURE ADR
          (      anyvariable : anytype (* in *) ) : ADDRESS;
(* Returns the address of any variable.                    *)

PROCEDURE SIZE
          (      anyvariable : anytype (* in *) ) : CARDINAL;
(* Returns the size, in bytes, of any variable.            *)

PROCEDURE TSIZE
          (      anytype1, anytype2, ..., ) : CARDINAL;
(* Returns the size, in bytes, of any type.                *)

PROCEDURE NEWPROCESS
          (      program    : PROC      (* in  *);
                 workspace  : ADDRESS   (* in  *);
                 spacesize  : CARDINAL  (* in  *);
             VAR newproc    : PROCESS   (* out *) );
(* Used to define a new coroutine.                         *)

PROCEDURE TRANSFER
          ( VAR oldprocess : PROCESS (* out    *);
            VAR newprocess : PROCESS (* in/out *) );
(* Used to transfer control from one coroutine to another.*)
```

**Figure 1.104**  Standard library module SYSTEM

## Type BYTE and WORD

The operation defined for types BYTE and WORD is assignment. Type BYTE may take on any value that occupies exactly one byte. Type WORD may take on any value that occupies exactly one word (machine dependent).

Objects of type BYTE or WORD are not compatible with other data types.

Some computers do not have byte-addressable memory; therefore, the BYTE type may not be available on such systems.

The size of a WORD varies from one machine to the next. A type transfer between a WORD type and any type that occupies one word of storage may be performed.

Formal procedure parameters such as ARRAY of BYTE and ARRAY of WORD may be bound to any arbitrary data type. This makes such procedure parameters extremely useful in writing generic software components.

## Type ADDRESS

Type ADDRESS is defined as:

```
TYPE ADDRESS = POINTER TO WORD;
```

Variables of type ADDRESS are compatible with all pointer types as well as the cardinal data type. The operations that may be performed on variables of type ADDRESS include pointer dereference, assignment, arithmetic, and relational operations.

A typical operation on address variables is address incrementation shown in Figure 1.105.

```
VAR adr : ADDRESS;

INC( adr, 10 * SIZE( WORD ) );
```

**Figure 1.105** Typical address incrementation

## *Hazard:*

Some computer systems place restrictions on address manipulations. On some byte-addressable machines, a word must begin at an even word boundary (i.e., an address that is a multiple of 2). On such a machine, it would not make sense to add one byte to an address. The resultant address would not point to a word.

## ADR Procedure

The procedure ADR operates on any variable and returns its address. Some examples are given in Figure 1.106.

```
VAR
    adr1, adr2 : ADDRESS;
    a          : ARRAY[ 1..100 ] OF INTEGER;
    r          : REAL;
BEGIN
  adr1 := ADR( a );
  adr2 := ADR( r );
```

**Figure 1.106** Examples of ADR operation

## SIZE and TSIZE Procedures

The procedures SIZE and TSIZE return the size, usually in bytes, of their argument. The argument of SIZE is always a variable, and the argument of TSIZE is always a data type.

If SIZE or TSIZE is used on a variant record variable or type, the value returned represents the largest field of the record.

## Examples of Low-level Bit Manipulation

Both examples presented in this section were developed and tested on an IBM PC AT using the Logitech Modula-2 system. Because of the low-level code, these procedures may require some modification in order to run in different hardware environments.

In Figure 1.107 some basic bit and byte manipulation procedures are presented.

```
PROCEDURE bitpattern
            (       item : WORD             (* in *) );
(*
   Writes the bit pattern of item to the screen.

   Input Parameters
   ----------------
   item - The one word entity to have its bitpattern
          displayed.
                                                        *)

VAR
     bit          : CARDINAL;

BEGIN
  FOR bit := 15 TO 0 BY -1 DO
    IF bit = 7
    THEN
      writestring( " | " );
    END(* if then *);
    IF bit IN BITSET( item )
    THEN
      write('1');
    ELSE
      write('0');
    END(* if then *);
  END(* for loop *);
  setmode( mode );
END bitpattern;
```

```
PROCEDURE shiftright
        (       item    : WORD       (* in *);
                nbits   : CARDINAL   (* in *) ) :
WORD;
(*
   Shifts the bits of item nbits to the right, replacing
   the bits with 0's.  The shifted item is returned.

   Input Parameters
   ----------------
   item  - The one word entity to have its bits shifted.
   nbits - The number of bits to shift the bits of item to
           the right.
                                                           *)

   VAR
       b               : BITSET;
       (* Input bit set  *)
       c               : BITSET;
       (* Output bit set *)
       pos             : CARDINAL;

BEGIN
  c := {};
  b := BITSET( item );
  FOR pos := nbits TO 15 DO
    IF pos IN b
    THEN
       INCL( c, pos - nbits );
    END(* if then *);
  END(* if then *);
  RETURN WORD( c );
END shiftright;

PROCEDURE shiftleft
        (       item : WORD              (* in     *);
               nbits   : CARDINAL        (* in     *) ) :
WORD;
(*
   Shifts the bits of item nbits to the left, replacing
   the bits with 0's.  The shifted item is returned.

   Input Parameters
   ----------------
   item  - The one word entity to have its bits shifted.
   nbits - The number of bits to shift the bits of item to
           the left.
                                                           *)

   VAR
       b                : BITSET;
       (* Input bit set  *)
       c                : BITSET;
       (* Output bit set *)
       pos              : CARDINAL;

BEGIN
  c := {};
  b := BITSET( item );
  FOR pos := 0 TO 15 - nbits DO
```

*(continued)*

```
        IF pos IN b
        THEN
          INCL( c, pos + nbits );
        END(* if then *);
     END(* for loop *);
   RETURN WORD( c );
END shiftleft;


PROCEDURE hibyte
     (     item   : WORD              (* in    *) ) ) :
WORD;
(*
   Returns the high byte of item as a word.

   Input Parameters
   ----------------
   item - The one word entity whose high byte is returned.
                                                          *)

   VAR
       b : WORD;

BEGIN
  b := shiftright( item, 8 );
  RETURN b;
END hibyte;


PROCEDURE lowbyte
     (     item   : WORD              (* in    *) ) ) :
WORD;
(*
   Returns the low byte of item as a word.

   Input Parameters
   ----------------
   item - The one word entity whose low byte is returned.
                                                          *)

   VAR
       b : WORD;

BEGIN
  b := shiftleft( item, 8 );
  b := shiftright( b, 8 );
  RETURN b;
END lowbyte;
```

**Figure 1.107**  Some basic bit manipulation procedures


In Figure 1.108, procedures define, push, and pop from the implementation module of a generic stack abstract data type are presented. Many of the important low-level operations presented earlier are used in procedures push and pop.

```
IMPLEMENTATION MODULE genericstack;
(* Some of the software engineers at Logitech Corp. are
   acknowledged for their help in refining this module.    *)

   FROM InOut IMPORT
     (* proc *) WriteLn, WriteString, WriteCard;

   FROM SYSTEM IMPORT
     (* type *) BYTE, ADDRESS,
     (* proc *) TSIZE;

   FROM Storage IMPORT
     (* proc *) ALLOCATE, DEALLOCATE;

   TYPE

        byteptr  = POINTER TO BYTE;

        address  = RECORD
                      CASE BOOLEAN OF
                        TRUE:  a: ADDRESS;
                        FALSE: b: byteptr;
                      END(* case *);
                   END(* record *);

        stack       = POINTER TO stackheader;

        stackptr    = POINTER TO stacknode;

        stackheader = RECORD
                         size   : CARDINAL;
                         next   : stackptr;
                      END (* record *);

        stacknode   = RECORD
                         contents : byteptr;
                         next     : stackptr;
                      END (* record *);

   PROCEDURE define
            ( VAR s : stack    (* out *) );

   BEGIN
     NEW( s );
     s^.size := 0;
     s^.next := NIL;
   END define;


   PROCEDURE push
            ( VAR s    : stack          (* in/out *);
                  item : ARRAY OF BYTE  (* in     *) );

   VAR
       size       : CARDINAL;
       newnode    : stackptr;
       bytecount  : CARDINAL;
       location   : address;
```

*(continued)*

```
BEGIN
  NEW ( newnode );
  (* Calculate size of item in bytes.                    *)
  size := ( HIGH( item ) + 1 );
  IF s^.size = 0
  THEN
    s^.size := size;
  ELSIF  s^.size # size
  THEN            (* The size of item is not compatible *)
    WriteLn;
    WriteString( "Error attempting to push an object " );
    WriteString( "of inconsistent size onto stack." );
    HALT; (* Stops program execution.                    *)
  END (* if then *);
  ALLOCATE( newnode^.contents, size );
  location.b := newnode^.contents;
  FOR bytecount := 0 TO HIGH( item ) DO
    location.b^ := item[ bytecount ];
    INC( location.a );
  END (* for loop *);
  newnode^.next := s^.next;
  s^.next := newnode;
END push;


PROCEDURE pop
          ( VAR s     : stack              (* in/out *);
            VAR item  : ARRAY OF BYTE       (* out     *) );

VAR
   size       : CARDINAL;
   oldnode    : stackptr;
   bytecount  : CARDINAL;
   location   : address;

BEGIN
  IF empty( s )
  THEN
    stackunderflow
  ELSE
    size       := s^.size;
    oldnode    := s^.next;
    location.b := oldnode^.contents;
    FOR bytecount := 0 TO size - 1 DO
      item[ bytecount ] := location.b^;
      INC( location.a );
    END (* for loop *);
    DEALLOCATE( oldnode^.contents, size );
    s^.next := oldnode^.next;
    DISPOSE( oldnode );
  END (* if then *)
END pop;

END genericstack.
```

**Figure 1.108** Segment of a generic stack package

## MS-DOS Specific Low-level Procedures

It is expected that every Modula-2 vendor will provide one or more library modules that provide the programmer with procedures that provide direct access to the underlying operating system.

### *Hazard:*

The use of operating-specific procedures assures that the resulting code is not portable between operating systems. Caution is therefore advised before using such procedures.

Figure 1.109 shows the MS-DOS specific constants and procedures provided by the Logitech Modula-2 system.

```
CONST
      AX, BX, CX, DX, SI, DI, ES, DS, CS, SS, SP, BP;
(* These constants denote the 8086 processor's
   registers.                                           *)

PROCEDURE GETREG
          (      register  : CARDINAL       (* in *);
              VAR value     : BYTE or WORD (* out *) );
(* Used to obtain the value stored in a register.      *)


PROCEDURE SETREG
          (      register : CARDINAL       (* in *);
                 value    : BYTE or WORD (* in *) );
(* Used to set the value in a register.                *)


PROCEDURE CODE
          ( code1const, code2const, ,,, : BYTE );


PROCEDURE SWI
          ( interruptvectornumber : CARDINAL );


PROCEDURE ENABLE;
(* Compiles to the assembly instruction STI.           *)


PROCEDURE DISABLE;
(* Compiles to the assembly instruction CLI.           *)
```

*(continued)*

```
PROCEDURE INBYTE
          (     port  : CARDINAL      (* in *);
              VAR value : BYTE or WORD (* out *) );
(* Get a byte value from the specified I/O port.      *)

PROCEDURE OUTBYTE
          (     port  : CARDINAL      (* in *);
                value : BYTE or WORD (* in *) );
(* Put a byte value to the specified I/O port.      *)

PROCEDURE INWORD
          (     port  : CARDINAL (* in *);
              VAR value : WORD       (* out *) );
(* Get a word value from the specified I/O port.      *)

PROCEDURE OUTWORD
          (     port  : CARDINAL (* in *);
                value : WORD       (* in *) );
(* Put a word value to the specified I/O port.      *)

PROCEDURE DOSCALL( functionnumber : CARDINAL; ... );
(* Used to access the predefined DOS calls provided by
   the operating system.                              *)
```

**Figure 1.109** MS DOS specific constants and procedures provided by Logitech

## Processes

In Module SYSTEM, a small number of low-level procedures are provided that support the process abstraction. This abstraction allows a programmer to specify various pseudoconcurrent tasks. In Modula-2, only pseudoconcurrent tasking is supported. There are no primitives available in current implementations that support true parallel processing with multiprocessors.

### Coroutines

When two or more procedures are defined with an equal relationship to each other (they share the processor on a time-sliced basis) they are called coroutines. None of the coroutine procedures are dominant either logically or with respect to the processor. They operate cooperatively. Any coroutine procedure can relinquish the processor to another coroutine procedure.

When a coroutine procedure resumes execution, it begins from where it previously relinquished control. If a coroutine procedure halts due to a fatal error before giving up control of the processor, all other coroutine procedures are stopped from gaining control, and the system crashes. True parallel processing cannot therefore be simulated in Modula-2 on a one-processor computer.

A coroutine procedure must be without parameters, at the outer level of nesting and is initiated by the NEWPROCESS procedure.

## PROCESS Type and NEWPROCESS Procedure

A process is associated with a parameterless procedure (coroutine procedure) declared at the outer level of scope in a program module. It cannot be contained within another procedure.

We invoke a process using procedure NEWPROCESS. Figure 1.110 shows the interface to this procedure.

```
PROCEDURE NEWPROCESS
        (       coroutine  : PROC    (* in *);
                workspace  : ADDRESS (* in *);
                sizespace  : CARDINAL (* in *);
            VAR newprocess : PROCESS (* out *) );
```

**Figure 1.110** Interface to NEWPROCESS procedure

The data type PROCESS is imported from module SYSTEM.

The coroutine parameter of procedure NEWPROCESS is the parameterless procedure not contained within another procedure.

The workspace parameter is the address of the area of memory used to store the stack of the process.

The sizespace parameter is the number of bytes available to the stack of the process.

The newprocess parameter is the process name associated with the coroutine procedure.

## *Software Engineering:*

An ordinary procedure is assigned memory workspace that is part of the stack space of its parent procedure (or main program). Because a process does not have a parent, its workspace must be explicitly allocated (using NEW or ALLOCATE) by the programmer.

The size of the workspace must be determined by trial and error. It must be large enough to hold all the variables defined in the process as well as procedure parameters internal to the coroutine procedure.

Many coroutine procedures (processes) are constructed using infinite loops. Within the loop the process may yield control to another process.

## TRANSFER Procedure

The interface to procedure TRANSFER is shown in Figure 1.111.

```
PROCEDURE TRANSFER
            ( VAR existingprocess : PROCESS (* in/out *);
              VAR newprocess      : PROCESS (* in/out *) );
```

**Figure 1.111** Interface to procedure TRANSFER

The parameter existingprocess is the process that is yielding control. The parameter newprocess is the process that is resuming control. Procedure TRANSFER is used by a coroutine procedure to yield control to another coroutine procedure.

## A Sample Process Abstraction

The interface to a typical process abstraction is given in Figure 1.112. The data structure for abstract data type SIGNAL and the implementation of the procedures send and wait are given in Figure 1.113.

```
TYPE SIGNAL;
(* Abstract data type used to enforce critical sections in
   coprocesses.                                           *)

TYPE processid
(* Descriptor of a process.                               *)


PROCEDURE startprocess
            (     p        : PROC          (* in *);
                  workspace : CARDINAL      (* in *);
                  name      : processname   (* in *) ;
```

```
PROCEDURE delay;
(* Puts a process at the back of the readyqueue of active
   processes.                                              *)


PROCEDURE destroysignal
           ( VAR s : signal (* in/out *) );
(* Releases all dynamically allocated storage associated
   with signal s.                                          *)


PROCEDURE equal
           ( p1, p2 : processid (* in *) );
(* Tests for the equality of process id's p1 and p2.       *)


PROCEDURE getprocessname
           ( VAR name : ARRAY OF CHAR (* out *) );
(* Returns the name assigned by the startprocess procedure
   to a coprocess or to the main program.                  *)


PROCEDURE init
           ( VAR s : signal (* out *) );
(* Initializes the description of the signal s.            *)


PROCEDURE numactiveproc() : CARDINAL;
(* Returns the number of currently active processes.       *)


PROCEDURE send
           ( VAR s : signal (* in/out *) );
(* Control is conditionally transferred to another
   process.                                                *)


PROCEDURE wait
           ( VAR s : signal (* in/out *) );
(* Suspends the current process until another process sends
   signal s.                                               *)


PROCEDURE sleep;
(* Suspends the main program until all coprocesses have
   terminated.                                             *)
```

**Figure 1.112** Interface to a process abstraction

```
TYPE signal    = POINTER TO semaphore;

     semaphore = RECORD
                    count : CARDINAL;
                    procs : queue;
                 END(* record *);

     processid  = POINTER TO descriptor;
```

*(continued)*

```
descriptor = RECORD
                 process       : PROCESS;
                 name          : processname;
                 parent        : processid;
                 workspace     : ADDRESS;
                 worspacesize  : CARDINAL;
             END(* record *);
PROCEDURE wait
          ( VAR s : signal (* in/out *) );

VAR
    prévprocess : processid;
    q           : queue;

BEGIN
  q := s^.procs;
  IF s^.count > 0
  THEN
    DEC( s^.count );
  ELSIF NOT empty( readyqueue )
  THEN
    insert( q, currentprocess );
    prevprocess := currentprocess;
    remove( readyqueue, currentprocess );
    TRANSFER( prevprocess^.process,
              currentprocess^.process );
  ELSE
    deadlockhandler; (* An error message indicating deadlock
                        is emitted. *)
  END(* if then *);
END wait;


PROCEDURE send
          ( VAR s : signal (* in/out *) );

VAR
   prevprocess : processid;
   q           : queue;

BEGIN
  q := s^.procs;
  IF NOT empty( q ) (* A process is waiting *)
  THEN
    insert( readyqueue, currentprocess );
    prevprocess := currentprocess;
    remove( q, currentprocess );
    TRANSFER( prevprocess^.process,
              currentprocess^.process );
```

```
    ELSE
      INC( s^.count );
      IF NOT empty( readyqueue )
      THEN
        insert( readyqueue, currentprocess );
        prevprocess := currentprocess;
        remove( readyqueue, currentprocess );
        TRANSFER( prevprocess^.process,
                  currentprocess^.process );
      END(* if then *);
    END(* if then *);
END send;
```

**Figure 1.113**  Implementation of parts of process abstraction

It is assumed that the abstract data type queue is available from an external module.

A process may send a signal to indicate that an event has occurred or may wait for a signal before commencing an event. This provides a way to ensure mutual exclusion (prevention of two coroutines from simultaneously attempting access or assignment to the same critical section of code). Each process sends a signal when leaving its own critical section and waits for a signal before entering its own critical section

The readyqueue, used in procedures send and wait, provides a mechanism for rapidly rotating through all the coroutines in a given system to create the illusion of simultaneous execution or parallel processing. (For a detailed discussion of the process abstraction see Ford, Wiener, *Modula-2: A Software Develpment Approach*, Chapter 16, Wiley, 1986.)

# Differences Between Pascal and Modula-2

- **Some Significant Differences**
- **Sample Programs Illustrating Some Differences**

## Some Significant Differences

The most significant differences between Pascal and Modula-2 relate to separate compilation, data hiding, low-level machine access, and coroutines. In addition, there are many small differences in syntax between Pascal and Modula-2.

The separate compilation feature of Modula-2 allows a programmer to separately compile three types of compilation units: definition modules, implementation modules, and program modules.

Abstract data types are encapsulated in a definition module. The body of the procedures and data structures for the abstract types are given in the implementation modules associated with each definition module. A powerful version control system that is part of every Modula-2 implementation assures that client modules must be recompiled when their parent modules are changed.

There is no counterpart to separate compilation in Pascal. Standard Pascal requires that an entire software system be contained within a single program. Pascal extensions such as UCSD™ Pascal allow for a limited form of independent compilation described below. No powerful version control systems exist for these extended Pascals.

Only a limited form of data hiding, the separation between the definition of a data type and its implementation, is possible in Pascal. In Pascal, a data type must be fully specified at its point of definition, thus making its data structure accessible throughout the Pascal program. In Modula-2, an opaque type's data structure is fully specified in the implementation module and is not accessible anyplace outside of the implementation module. This enforces consistency of usage among the procedures and modules that comprise a Modula-2 software system.

Although low-level machine access is not defined in standard Pascal, some recent implementations of Pascal have extended the language to include some bit and byte manipulations.

The process abstraction using coroutines is not specified in standard Pascal. Some limited binary semaphore capabilities have been provided in some recent and nonstandard versions of Pascal.

In UCSD Pascal, developed at the University of California in the 1970s, a compilation unit called the UNIT is defined. This independent compilation unit contains both an interface portion as well as implementation portion.

The implementation portion of the UNIT contains the body of all the procedures that are part of the interface. The interface portion must fully specify the data structures of all data types defined in this section. Thus these implementation details are accessible everywhere outside such a UNIT. It is possible in UCSD Pascal to have private data types and procedures that do not appear in the interface portion of the UNIT. These are not accessible outside of the UNIT. Since they do not appear in the interface portion, they are of value only to the implementation portion of the UNIT and are useless outside the UNIT.

Figure 2.1 summarizes some deficiencies found in Pascal that have been corrected in Modula-2.

1. No facilities are provided for separate compilation. This makes problem decomposition and team programming difficult.

2. No facilities are provided for separating the definition of a data type from its implementation. This makes it impossible to employ some modern and effective software engineering methodologies such as object-oriented design because of the lack of support for data hiding.

3. No facilities for coroutines. This makes it difficult to write interrupt handling routines. It is not possible to design software that exploits the process abstraction.

4. Procedure parameters must always be bound to actual parameters of the same type. This makes it impossible to write generic procedures containing generic parameters.

5. Variables that stay alive for the full duration of a program must be global. This makes such variables accessible everywhere and vulnerable to corruption.

6. The short-circuiting of boolean expressions is not specified. This results in the necessity to occassionally write cumbersome code.

7. The case construct does not have an else clause. This can result in serious case tag errors at run-time.

8. The declaration order for constants, types, variables, and procedures is rigidly prescribed. This makes it difficult to declare an entity near its point of application.

9. Type transfer is not defined.

*(continued)*

10. The input and output procedures that are predefined cannot be changed or customized. This severely limits the range of input and output facilities that are possible.

11. Low-level access to the bits and bytes of the machine are not provided in standard Pascal.

**Figure 2.1** Some deficiencies in Pascal that have been corrected in Modula-2

## Sample Programs Illustrating Some Differences

Figure 2.2 compares a Pascal program with its Modula-2 counterpart to illustrate the difference between branching constructs in the two languages. The Pascal program requires the frequent use of begin statements to allow for the blocks of code after then statements and else statements. These are not required in Modula-2. Modula-2's ELSIF statement streamlines the logic.

```
program compare1;

var
    j, k, : integer;

begin
  j := 16;
  k := 12;
  if k > j
  then begin
    writeln;
    writeln( 'k > j.' );
  end
  else begin
    if k = j
    then begin
      writeln;
      writeln( 'k = j.' );
    end
    else begin
      writeln;
      writeln( 'k < j.' );
    end;
  end;
end.


MODULE compare1;

  FROM InOut IMPORT
    (* proc *) WriteLn, WriteString;

  VAR
      j, k : INTEGER;

BEGIN
  j := 16;
  k := 12;
  IF k > j
```

```
THEN
  WriteLn;
  WriteString( "k > j." );
  WriteLn;
ELSIF k = j
THEN
  WriteLn;
  WriteString( "k = j." );
  WriteLn;
ELSE
  WriteLn;
  WriteString( "k < j." );
  WriteLn;
END(* if then *);
END compare1.
```

**Figure 2.2** Comparison of Pascal and Modula-2 programs

Figure 2.3 compares another Pascal program with its Modula-2 counterpart to illustrate the difference between FOR loops and WHILE loops.

```
program compare2;

var
    i, j : integer;

begin
  j := 0;
  for i := 10 downto 1 do begin
    j := j + 1;
    j := j + i;
  end;
  j := 10;
  i := 4;
  while ( i < j ) do
    j := j - 2;
end.


MODULE compare2;

VAR
    i, j : INTEGER;

BEGIN
  j := 0;
  FOR i := 10 TO 1 BY -1 DO
    INC( j );
    INC( j, i );
  END(* for loop *);
  j := 10;
  i := 4;
  WHILE ( i < j ) DO
    DEC( j, 2 );
  END(* while loop *);
END compare2.
```

**Figure 2.3** Comparison of Pascal and Modula-2 programs

Figure 2.4 again compares another Pascal program with its Modula-2 counterpart to illustrate short circuiting of Boolean expressions.

```
program compare3;

var
     pos : integer;

begin
  pos := 1;
  while ( pos < 1000 ) and ( a[ pos ] <> key ) do
    pos := pos + 1;
  if a[ pos ] <> key
  then
    pos := 1001;
  compare3 := pos;
end.


MODULE compare3;

VAR
     pos : INTEGER;

BEGIN
  pos := 1;
  WHILE ( pos <= 1000 ) AND ( a[ pos ] # key ) DO
    INC( pos );
  END(* while loop *);
  RETURN pos;
END compare3.
```

**Figure 2.4**  Comparison of Pascal and Modula-2 programs

Figure 2.5 compares one last Pascal program with its Modula-2 counterpart to illustrate the difference between CASE statements.

```
program compare4;

var
   i, j, k : integer;

begin
  i := 5;
  j := 7;
  k := i + j;
  writeln( 'k = ', k );
  writeln( 'i = ', i );
  if i <= 7 then
    case i of
      1 : write( 'Case 1.' );
      2 : write( 'Case 1.' );
      3 : write( 'Case 1.' );
      4 : write( 'Case 1.' );
      5 : write( 'Case 2.' );
      6 : write( 'Case 3.' );
      7 : write( 'Case 3.' );
    end(* case *)
```

```
    else
      write( 'Case 4.' );
  end.


  MODULE compare4;

    FROM InOut IMPORT
      (* proc *) WriteLn, WriteString, WriteInt,
                  WriteCard;

    VAR
        i, j : INTEGER;
        k      : CARDINAL;

  BEGIN
    i := 5;
    j := 7;
    k := CARDINAL( i ) + CARDINAL( j );
    WriteString( "k = " );
    WriteCard( k, 1 );
    WriteLn;
    WriteString( "i = " );
    WriteInt( i, 1 );
    WriteLn;
    CASE i OF
      1..4 :
        WriteString( "Case 1." );  |
      5    :
        WriteString( "Case 2." );  |
      6..7 :
        WriteString( "Case 3." );
    ELSE
      WriteString( "Case 4." );
    END(* case *);
  END compare4.
```

**Figure 2.5** Comparison of Pascal and Modula-2 programs

# SECTION 3

# Input and Output

- **The Standardization of Modula-2 Libraries**
- **Module InOut**
- **New Standard Input/Output Libraries**
- **Customized Input/Output: Module Termio**

# The Standard-ization of Modula-2 Libraries

As in C, all of Modula-2's support for terminal and file input and output is relegated to external library modules. A library module InOut has been supplied with virtually all Modula-2 systems. This module contains procedures for reading and writing data to a video terminal as well as a text file stream. At the time of this writing, most vendors are still supplying this module, but this may change.

There has been a justifiable concern in the Modula-2 community about the issue of standardization. The concern has focused not on the language but on the libraries supporting the language.

In an effort to standardize Modula-2 libraries, the Modula-2 User Association, with input from the prominent Modula-2 vendors, published a proposed standard for important library modules in *MODUS*, Quarterly Issue #1, Jan. 1985. The proposal was made by an ad-hoc committee chaired by Randy Bush (Pacific Systems Group) and including Svend Knudsen (ETH Zurich), Anton Gorrengourt (Logitech), Alfred Moertelseder (Logitech), Willy Steiger (Logitech), Leo Geissman, Jirka Hoppe, and Joel McCormack (Volition Systems).

The goals of the MODUS group are listed in Figure 3.1.

```
1.  To support portability between Modula-2 systems.

2.  Provide the basis for writing software tools.

3.  Allow one to describe algorithms that refer to a
    standard environment.

4.  Make the standard library independent of the operating
    system.

5.  Provide Pascal-like facilities for the beginning
    programmer.

6.  Provide the experienced programmer more control.

7.  Do not preclude the addition of environment dependent
    features (e.g. tasking, exceptions, ... ).

8.  Do not attempt to provide portability of data files
    between implementations but only portability of
    functionality.
```

**Figure 3.1** The goals of MODUS in standardizing Modula-2 libraries

The author is grateful to the Logitech Corp, 805 Veterans Boulevard, Redwood City, Ca. 94063 for providing an early beta test copy of the new standard Modula-2 library and for giving their permission to publish it here. Although some of the details may have changed slightly by the time this book is published, it is expected that the current version is close to final. The reader is encouraged to check with Logitech or MODUS for the latest details.

This section includes the interface (definition module) for module InOut and the interface to the new standard input/output libraries as supplied by Logitech, Inc. with their permission. It is expected that the new standard will gradually replace the old InOut.

## Module InOut

Figure 3.2 shows the Logitech definition module for InOut. Documentation for using this module is provided in the form of embedded comments given by Logitech.

```
DEFINITION MODULE InOut;

  FROM SYSTEM IMPORT
    (* type *) WORD;

  FROM FileSystem IMPORT
    (* type *) File;

  EXPORT QUALIFIED
    EOL, Done, in, out, termCH,
    OpenInput, OpenOutput, CloseInput, CloseOutput,
    Read, ReadString, ReadInt, ReadCard, ReadWrd,
    Write, WriteLn, WriteString, WriteInt, WriteCard,
    WriteOct, WriteHex, WriteWrd;


  CONST
    EOL = 36C;
    (* End-of-line character.                          *)


  VAR
    Done:  BOOLEAN;
    (* Set by several procedures; TRUE if the
       operation was successful, FALSE otherwise.      *)

    termCH:  CHAR;
    (* Terminating character from ReadString, ReadInt,
       ReadCard.                                       *)

    in, out: File;
    (* The currently open input and output files.
       Use for exceptional cases only.                 *)
```

*(continued)*

```
PROCEDURE OpenInput
        (    defext : ARRAY OF CHAR (* in *) );
(* Accept a file name from the terminal and open it for
   input (file variable 'in').

in:    defext  default filetype or 'extension'.

If the file name that is read doesn't end with '.', and it
doesn't have an extension, then 'defext' is appended to
the file name.

If OpenInput succeeds, Done = TRUE and subsequent input is
taken from the file until CloseInput is called.
                                                          *)


PROCEDURE OpenOutput
        (    defext : ARRAY OF CHAR (* in *) );
(* Accept a file name from the terminal and open it for
   output (file variable 'out').

in:    defext  default filetype or 'extension'.

If the file name that is read doesn't end with '.', and it
doesn't have an extension, then 'defext' is appended to
the file name.

If OpenOutput succeeds, Done = TRUE and subsequent output
is written to the file until CloseOutput is called.

                                                          *)


PROCEDURE CloseInput;
(* Close current input file and revert to terminal for
   input.                                                 *)


PROCEDURE CloseOutput;
(*  Close current output file and revert to terminal for
    output.                                               *)


PROCEDURE Read
        ( VAR ch : CHAR (* out *) );
(* Read the next character from the current input.

out:    ch     the character read; EOL for end-of-line

Done = TRUE unless the input is at end of file.           *)


PROCEDURE ReadString
        ( VAR s : ARRAY OF CHAR (* out *) );
(* Read a string from the current input.

out:    s      the string that was read, excluding
               the terminator character.

Leading blanks are accepted and thrown away, then
characters are read into 's' until a blank or control
character is entered. ReadString truncates the input
string if it is too long for 's'. The terminating
character is left in 'termCH'. If input is from the
terminal, BS and DEL are allowed for editing.            *)
```

```
PROCEDURE ReadInt
          ( VAR x : INTEGER (* out *) );
(* Read an INTEGER representation from the current input.

out:    x       the value read.

ReadInt is like ReadString, but the string is converted to
an INTEGER value if possible, using the syntax:
["+"|"-"] digit { digit }.
Done = TRUE if some conversion took place.              *)


PROCEDURE ReadCard
          ( VAR x : CARDINAL (* out *) );
(* Read an unsigned decimal number from the current input.

out:    x       the value read.

ReadCard is like ReadInt, but the syntax is:
digit { digit }.                                        *)


PROCEDURE ReadWrd
          ( VAR w : WORD (* out *) );
(* Read a WORD value from the current input.

out:    w       the value read.

Done is TRUE if a WORD was read successfully. This
procedure cannot be used when reading from the terminal.
Note that the meaning of WORD is system dependent.      *)


PROCEDURE Write
          (   ch : CHAR (* in *) );
(* Write a character to the current output.

in:    ch       character to write.                     *)


PROCEDURE WriteLn;
(* Write an end-of-line sequence to the current output. *)


PROCEDURE WriteString
          (   s : ARRAY OF CHAR (* in *) );
(* Write a string to the current output.

in:    s        string to write.                        *)


PROCEDURE WriteInt
          (   x : INTEGER (* in *);
              n : CARDINAL(* in *) );
(* Write an integer in right-justified decimal format.

in:    x        value to be output,
       n        minimum field width.
```

The decimal representation of 'x' (including '-' if x is
negative) is output, using at least n characters (but

*(continued)*

```
more if needed). Leading blanks are output if
necessary.                                            *)


PROCEDURE WriteCard
           (     x, n : CARDINAL (* in *) );
(* Output a CARDINAL in decimal format.

in:     x          value to be output,
        n          minimum field width.

The decimal representation of the value 'x' is output,
using at least n characters (but more if needed).
Leading blanks are output if necessary.               *)


PROCEDURE WriteOct
           (     x, n : CARDINAL (* in *) );
(* Output a CARDINAL in octal format.
   [see WriteCard above].                             *)


PROCEDURE WriteHex
           (     x, n : CARDINAL (* in *) );
(* Output a CARDINAL in hexadecimal format.

in:     x          value to be output,
        n          minimum field width.

Four uppercase hex digits are written, with leading
blanks if n > 4.                                      *)


PROCEDURE WriteWrd
           (    w : WORD (* in *) );
(* Output a WORD

in:     w          WORD value to be output.

Note that the meaning of WORD is system dependent, and
that a WORD cannot be written to the terminal.        *)


END InOut.
```

**Figure 3.2** Logitech's InOut module


## New Standard Input/Output Libraries

The following standard libraries are provided by Logitech and are reproduced with their permission.

In Figure 3.3, module StandardIO is given. The comments are given by Logitech.

```
DEFINITION MODULE StandardIO;

  FROM Files IMPORT File;

  EXPORT QUALIFIED
      SetInput,        GetInput,        SetOutput,  GetOutput,
      EchoMode,        SetEchoMode,     GetEchoMode,
      GetErrorInput,   GetErrorOutput,
      LogMode,         SetLogMode,      GetLogMode,
      SetLog,          GetLog;

  (* Standard system input and output files.              *)

  PROCEDURE SetInput       (      input      : File );
  (* Sets the standard input to the value of input.       *)

  PROCEDURE GetInput       ( VAR input       : File );
  (* Gets the current handle for the standard input File. *)

  PROCEDURE SetOutput      (      output     : File );
  (* Sets the standard output to the value of Output.     *)

  PROCEDURE GetOutput      ( VAR output      : File );
  (* Gets the current handle for the standard output File.*)

  (* Control of echoing from standard input to standard
     output.                                              *)

  TYPE
      EchoMode = (echo, noEcho);

  PROCEDURE SetEchoMode    (      mode       : EchoMode);
  (* If "mode" is "echo", causes the standard input to be
     echoed to the current standard output file.          *)

  PROCEDURE GetEchoMode    ()                : EchoMode;
  (* Returns the current value of echo mode.              *)

  PROCEDURE GetErrorOutput ( VAR errorFile   : File );
  (* Error output is the file to which error messages are
     sent.                                                *)

  PROCEDURE GetErrorInput  ( VAR errorFile   : File );
  (* Error input is the file to which a user must respond
     after an error has occured ("press <space> to
     continue"). Abort, Retry, Ignore.                    *)

  (* Chars written or echoed to the Output file may be
     copied to the Log file.  This allows input to be
     copied to two output files for "photo sessions"      *)

  TYPE
      LogMode = (loggingOn, loggingOff);

  PROCEDURE SetLog         (      log        : File);
```

*(continued)*

```
        PROCEDURE GetLog          ( VAR log          : File );

        PROCEDURE SetLogMode      (      mode         : LogMode);

        PROCEDURE GetLogMode      ()                  : LogMode;

    END StandardIO.
```

**Figure 3.3**  Standard input/output module StandardIO

In Figure 3.4, module SimpleIO is given. The comments are given by Logitech and the module reproduced with their permission.

```
DEFINITION MODULE SimpleIO;
(* Uses the "standard" files input, output, and log
   which may be manipulated by the module StandardIO.     *)

  FROM SYSTEM IMPORT WORD;

  EXPORT QUALIFIED
      EOT,        EOL,
      ReadChar,  ReadString,  ReadLn,  ReadInt,  ReadCard,
      ReadNum, CondRead,  UndoRead,
      WriteChar, WriteString, WriteLn, WriteInt, WriteCard,
      WriteNum;

  PROCEDURE EOT         ()              : BOOLEAN;

  PROCEDURE EOL         ()              : BOOLEAN;

  PROCEDURE ReadChar    (VAR ch    : CHAR);

  PROCEDURE ReadString (VAR str  : ARRAY OF CHAR);

  PROCEDURE ReadLn;

  PROCEDURE ReadInt     (VAR int     : INTEGER;
                         VAR success : BOOLEAN);

  PROCEDURE ReadCard    (VAR card    : CARDINAL;
                         VAR success : BOOLEAN);

  PROCEDURE ReadNum     (VAR num     : WORD;
                             base    : CARDINAL(* [2..36] *);
                         VAR success : BOOLEAN);

  PROCEDURE CondRead    (VAR ch      : CHAR;
                         VAR success : BOOLEAN);

  PROCEDURE UndoRead    ();

  PROCEDURE WriteChar   (      ch    : CHAR);

  PROCEDURE WriteLn;

  PROCEDURE WriteString(      str    : ARRAY OF CHAR);

  PROCEDURE WriteInt    (      int   : INTEGER;
                               width : CARDINAL);
```

```
PROCEDURE WriteCard   (   card   : CARDINAL;
                          width  : CARDINAL);

PROCEDURE WriteNum    (   num    : WORD;
                          base   : CARDINAL(* [2..36] *);
                          width  : CARDINAL);

END SimpleIO.
```

**Figure 3.4** Standard input/output module SimpleIO

In Figure 3.5, module Terminal is given. The comments are given by Logitech and the module reproduced with their permission.

```
DEFINITION MODULE Terminal;
(* Bypasses the file system, permitting rapid and direct
   access to the console device.  It is useful to programs
   which are written to be embedded or screen oriented
   applications.                                          *)

EXPORT QUALIFIED
    ReadChar,    ReadString,   CondRead,
    WriteChar,   WriteString,  WriteLn,
    NumRows,     NumCols,      GotoRowCol,
    EraseScreen, EraseToEOL,   EraseToEOS;

PROCEDURE ReadChar     (VAR ch     : CHAR);    (* echo *)

PROCEDURE ReadString   (VAR str    : ARRAY OF CHAR);
(* until EOL or EOS.                                     *)

PROCEDURE CondRead(     VAR ch     : CHAR; (* no echo *)
                        VAR success : BOOLEAN);
(* if not, ch := undef                                   *)

PROCEDURE WriteChar    (    ch     : CHAR);

PROCEDURE WriteString  (    str    : ARRAY OF CHAR);

PROCEDURE WriteLn;

PROCEDURE NumRows      ()           : CARDINAL;
(* Size of screen.                                       *)

PROCEDURE NumCols      ()           : CARDINAL;

PROCEDURE GotoRowCol (     row    : CARDINAL;
                           col    : CARDINAL);
(*  0, 0 is top of screen.                               *)

PROCEDURE EraseScreen;

PROCEDURE EraseToEOL;
(* From cursor to eol.                                   *)

PROCEDURE EraseToEOS;
(* From cursor to eos.                                   *)

END Terminal.
```

**Figure 3.5** Standard input/output module Terminal

In Figure 3.6, module Text is given. The comments are given by Logitech and the module reproduced with their permission.

```
DEFINITION MODULE Text;

  FROM Files IMPORT File, FileState;

  EXPORT QUALIFIED
      EOL,
      ReadChar,        ReadLn,          ReadString,
      UndoRead,        CondRead,
      WriteChar,       WriteString,   WriteLn;


  PROCEDURE EOL        ( file      : File)
                                   : BOOLEAN;
  (* Returns true if last operation was not performed due
     to end of line or error.                          *)

  PROCEDURE ReadChar ( file      : File;
                       VAR ch       : CHAR;
                       VAR state    : FileState);
  (* Read a char from a TextFile.  If the file is the
     standard input file, then echoing is controlled by
     module StandardIO.                                 *)

  PROCEDURE ReadString(file      : File;
                       VAR str      : ARRAY OF CHAR;
                       VAR state    : FileState);
  (* Read a string from a text file until EOL,
     EOF, or end of string.                             *)

  PROCEDURE ReadLn   ( file      : File;
                       VAR state    : FileState);
  (* Eat characters until EOL, then eat EOL.            *)

  PROCEDURE UndoRead(  file      : File;
                       VAR state    : FileState);
  (* Allow most recently read CHAR to be read again.    *)

  PROCEDURE CondRead(  file      : File;
                       VAR ch       : CHAR;
                       VAR success : BOOLEAN;
                       VAR state    : FileState);
  (* Attempt to read a char: return TRUE in "success" if
     read succeeds; return FALSE in "success" if read
     fails.  If read fails, value in "ch" is undefined.  *)

  PROCEDURE WriteChar( file      : File;
                       ch        : CHAR;
                       VAR state    : FileState);
  (* Write a single character to a text file.           *)

  PROCEDURE WriteString(file      : File;
                        str       : ARRAY OF CHAR;
                        VAR state    : FileState);
  (* Write a string of characters to a text file.       *)
```

```
     PROCEDURE WriteLn  ( file    : File;
                          VAR state  : FileState);
     (* Write an EOL to a text file.                    *)

END Text.
```

**Figure 3.6** Standard input/output module Text

In Figure 3.7, module Files is given. The comments are given by Logitech and the module reproduced with their permission.

```
DEFINITION MODULE Files;

    EXPORT QUALIFIED
        File,          FileState,
        BinTextMode,   ReadWriteMode,  ReplaceMode,
        Open,          Create,         Close,          Remove,
        Reset,         Rewrite,        Truncate,       Flush,
        EOF,           State,          ResetState,
        GetFileName;

    TYPE
        Filc;
        BinTextMode   = (binMode, textMode);
        ReadWriteMode = (readOnly, readWrite, appendOnly);
        ReplaceMode   = (noReplace, replace);

        FileState = (
        ok,          (* errors opening files                    *)
        nameError,(* Illegal syntax in file name as passed *)
        noFile,      (* file with specified name not found     *)
        existingFile,(* file already exists                    *)
                     (* errors opening or operating            *)
        deviceError, (* some hardware error during I/O         *)
        noMoreRoom,  (* no room on volume/medium/directory *)
        accessError, (* protect, read/write, binary/text
                        error                                  *)
                     (* errors operating upon a file           *)
        notOpen,     (* operation on unopened file             *)
        endError,    (* read attempted after EOL or EOF        *)
        outsideFile, (* position before BOF or after EOF       *)
                     (* and *)
        otherError   (* error unanticipated by this
                        definition                             *)
                     );
    PROCEDURE Open      (VAR file    : File;
                         name       : ARRAY OF CHAR;
                         binText    : BinTextMode;
                         writeMode  : ReadWriteMode;
                         VAR state  : FileState);
    (* Open an existing external file; error if not present.*)
```

*(continued)*

```
PROCEDURE Create  (VAR file     : File;
                       name      : ARRAY OF CHAR;
                       binText   : BinTextMode;
                       replMode  : ReplaceMode;
                   VAR state    , : FileState);
(* Create a new external file.  If named file already
   exists, then overwrite only if replMode = replace,
   otherwise, error.                                  *)

PROCEDURE Close   (VAR file     : File;
                   VAR state     : FileState);
(* Close the file, saving the external file.          *)

PROCEDURE Remove  (VAR file     : File;
                   VAR state     : FileState);
(* Close the file, removing the external file.        *)

PROCEDURE Reset   (   file      : File;
                   VAR state     : FileState);
(* Reposition to the start of the file.               *)

PROCEDURE Rewrite (   file      : File;
                   VAR state     : FileState);
(* Reposition to start of file and then truncate file. *)

PROCEDURE Truncate (  file      : File;
                   VAR state     : FileState);
(* Set the end of the file to the current position.   *)

PROCEDURE Flush   (   file      : File;
                   VAR state     : FileState);
(* Writes any modified buffers to the storage medium.  *)

PROCEDURE EOF     (   file      : File)
                                : BOOLEAN;
(* Returns true if last operation was not performed due
   to end of file or error.                           *)

PROCEDURE State   (  file       : File)
                                : FileState;
(* Returns the current state of the file.             *)

PROCEDURE ResetState ( file      : File;
                   VAR state     : FileState);
(* Allows continued operation in presence of error
   conditions; reevaluates EOF/EOL so that they really
   indicate file position.                            *)

PROCEDURE GetFileName ( file     : File;
                   VAR name      : ARRAY OF CHAR;
                   VAR state     : FileState);
(* Returns the complete and unambiguous name of the
   file.                                              *)

END Files.
```

**Figure 3.7** Standard input/output module Files

## Customized Input/Output: Module termio

The modules presented earlier do not provide support for many practical terminal input/output functions. Module termio, developed by the author, defines a large set of descriptive constants for every key on an IBM PC keyboard for use with the input procedure read. Using termio's read, it is easy to trap any keyboard input. Many of the procedures given in InOut and the standard libraries are not fully error-protected against erroneous input such as character input when a number is expected, or numbers that cause overflow errors.

Module termio, written for MS-DOS systems and tested under the Logitech Modula-2 system, is a general purpose, powerful, and customized terminal input/output package. Its implementation illustrates many useful low-level features of Modula-2 running under MS-DOS, including in-line assembly code.

Figure 3.8 gives the definition module for module termio. It contains extensive documentation in the form of embedded comments. The author thanks Steve Mahone for his help in developing this module.

```
DEFINITION MODULE termio;

(*
   This package of terminal input/output procedures re-
   places much of Logitech's modules InOut. The write modes
   of normal, reverse, and underline may be set for any
   output to the screen.  Extensive error protection is
   built into the input procedures.
                                                         *)

   EXPORT QUALIFIED

     (* Function keys *)
     F1, F2, F3, F4, F5, F6, F7, F8, F9, F10,

     (* Control keys *)
     ctla, ctlb, ctlc, ctld, ctle, ctlf, ctlg, ctlj,
     ctlk, ctll, ctln, ctlo, ctlp, ctlq, ctlr, ctls,
     ctlt, ctlu, ctlv, ctlw, ctlx, ctly, ctlz,

     (* Other keys *)
     ua, da,           (* uparrow and downarrow          *)
     ra, la,           (* rightarrow and leftarrow       *)
     pu, pd,           (* pageup and pagedn              *)
     hm, en,           (* home and end                   *)
     bs, del,          (* backspace and delete           *)
```

*(continued)*

```
    tab, stab,        (* tab and shift-tab                 *)
    ins, ret,         (* toggle ins and screen carr ret    *)

    (* const *)
    cr, lf, eof,      (* carr ret, linefeed, end of file   *)
    bkch, esc, nul,   (* blank char, escape, null          *)

    (* type *) modetype,

    (* proc *) readstring, readint, readcard, read,
               echoread, writestring, writeint, writecard,
               repeatwrite, write, writeln, setmode,
               getmode, right, left, up, down, gotoxy,
               getxy, clrtoeol, clrscreen, spacebar,
               centermessage, yes;

CONST
    F1 = 128; F2 = 129; F3 = 130; F4 = 131; F5  = 132;
    F6 = 133; F7 = 134; F8 = 135; F9 = 136; F10 = 137;

    ctla = 138; ctlb = 139; ctlc = 140; ctld = 141;
    ctle = 142; ctlf = 143; ctlg = 144; ctlj = 145;
    ctlk = 146; ctll = 147; ctln = 148; ctlo = 149;
    ctlp = 150; ctlq = 151; ctlr = 152;
    ctls = 153; ctlt = 154; ctlu = 155;
    ctlv = 156; ctlw = 157; ctlx = 158;
    ctly = 159; ctlz = 160;

    ua = 161; da = 162; ra  = 163; la  = 164; pu  = 165;
    pd = 166; hm = 167; en  = 168; del = 169; stab = 170;
    ret= 171; bs = 8;   tab = 9;

    nul = 0C;  lf  = 12C; cr   = 15C;
    eof = 32C; esc = 33C; bkch = 40C;

TYPE modetype = ( normal, reverse, underline, highlight );
(* Used to control the type of printing on the screen.  *)




VAR
    ins : BOOLEAN;  (* is toggled by read *)


PROCEDURE gotoxy
         (     x, y : CARDINAL                 (* in *) );
(*
    The cursor is moved to column x and row y.
    The cursor is not moved if x is out of range (0..79)
    or if y is out of range (0..24).  The value x = 79 and
    y = 24 is not allowed.

    Input Parameters
    ----------------
    x - The cursor is placed in column x ( 0..79).
    y - The cursor is placed in row y (0..24).
                                                        *)
```

```
PROCEDURE clrtoeol;

(*
   The screen is cleared from the cursor position to the
   end of the line.
                                                            *)

PROCEDURE getxy
           ( VAR x, y : CARDINAL           (* out *) );
(*
   Returns the x (column) and y (row ) position of the
   cursor.

   Output Parameters
   -----------------
   x - The column position of the cursor ( 0..79 ).
   y - The row position of the cursor ( 0..24 ).
                                                            *)

PROCEDURE right
           (      x  : CARDINAL            (* in *) );
(*
   Moves the cursor x places to the right. The cursor is
   not moved if the value of x would move the cursor off
   the screen.

   Input Parameters
   ----------------
   x - Moves the cursor x spaces to the right.
                                                            *)

PROCEDURE left
           (      x  : CARDINAL            (* in *) );

(*
   Moves the cursor x places to the left. The cursor is
   not moved if the value of x would move the cursor off
   the screen.

   Input Parameters
   ----------------
   x - Moves the cursor x spaces to the left.
                                                            *)

PROCEDURE up
           (      x  : CARDINAL            (* in *) );

(*
   Moves the cursor x places up. The cursor is not moved
   if the value of x would move the cursor off the screen.

   Input Parameters
   ----------------
   x - Moves the cursor x spaces up.
                                                            *)

PROCEDURE down
           (      x  : CARDINAL            (* in *) );
```

*(continued)*

```
(*
   Moves the cursor x places down. The cursor is not moved
   if the value of x would move the cursor off the screen.

   Input Parameters
   ----------------
   x - Moves the cursor x spaces down.
                                                            *)

PROCEDURE clrscreen;
(*
   Clears the screen and puts the cursor in the home
   position.
                                                            *)

PROCEDURE setmode
            (    m  : modetype              (* in *) );
(*
   Used to set the mode for writing output to the screen.
   The choices for m are normal, reverse, underline, or
   highlight.  The default mode is set to normal.

   Input Parameters
   ----------------
   m - Used to set the screen for normal, reverse,
       underline or highlight.
                                                            *)


PROCEDURE getmode
            ( VAR m  : modetype              (* out *) );
(*
   Returns the current mode for writing output to the
   screen.  The choices are normal, reverse, underline,
   or highlight.

   Output Parameters
   ----------------
   m - Returns the current video mode.
                                                            *)

PROCEDURE readstring
            ( VAR s  : ARRAY OF CHAR         (* out *) );
(*
   Returns string s input from the keyboard. Carriage
   return (CR) is used as a terminator.  The backspace key
   may be used to erase characters.  The input string is
   truncated if it is too long.

   Output Parameters
   ----------------
   s - Returns the string, s, input from keyboard.
                                                            *)


PROCEDURE readint
            ( VAR i  : INTEGER               (* out *) );
(*
   Returns integer i input from the keyboard.  Carriage
   return (CR) is used as a terminator.  Only numerals may
   be input except that a negative sign may be used as the
   first character input.  The backspace key may be used
   to erase characters.  The largest absolute value of
```

integer that may be entered is 32767. Larger absolute
values are rejected by putting the cursor back to its
starting point after erasing the illegal input.

Output Parameters
-----------------
i - Returns the integer, i, input from the keyboard.
                                                        *)

PROCEDURE readcard
        ( VAR c  : CARDINAL              (* out *) );
(*
  Returns cardinal c input from the keyboard.  Carriage
  return (CR) is used as a terminator.  Only numerals may
  be input.  The backspace key may be used to erase
  characters.  The largest value of cardinal that
  may be entered is 65535.  Larger values are rejected by
  putting the cursor back to its starting point after
  erasing the illegal input.

  Output Parameters
  -----------------
  c - Returns the cardinal, c, input from the keyboard.
                                                        *)

PROCEDURE read
        ( VAR ch : CHAR                  (* out *) );
(*
  Returns the character ch input from the keyboard
  without echo.

  Output Parameters
  -----------------
  ch - Returns the character, ch, input from the
       keyboard, without echo. Any character from the
       keyboard may be input.  The constants defined
       above allow each possible key to be
       referenced symbolically.
                                                        *)

PROCEDURE echoread
        ( VAR ch : CHAR                  (* out *) );
(*
  Returns the character ch input from the keyboard with
  echo.

  Output Parameters
  -----------------
  ch - Same as read except for echo from the keyboard.
                                                        *)

PROCEDURE writestring
        (     s  : ARRAY OF CHAR         (* in *) );

(*
  Writes the string s to the screen.

  Input Parameters
  -----------------
  s - String s is written to the screen.
                                                        *)

*(continued)*

```
PROCEDURE write
              (       ch : CHAR                        (* in *) );
(*
   Writes the character ch to the screen.  Hidden control
   characters may be written to the screen.

   Input Parameters
   ----------------
   ch - Character ch is written to the screen.
                                                              *)

PROCEDURE repeatwrite
              (       ch      : CHAR                   (* in *);
                      numrep : CARDINAL                (* in *) );
(*
   Writes ch to the screen numrep times very rapidly.

   Input Parameters
   ----------------
   ch      - Character written very rapidly to the screen
             numrep times.
   numrep - The number of times character ch is written to
             the screen.
                                                              *)

PROCEDURE writeln;
(*
   The cursor is advanced to the leftmost position of
   the next line.
                                                              *)

PROCEDURE writeint
              (       i      : INTEGER                 (* in *);
                      width : CARDINAL                 (* in *) );
(*
   Writes integer i to the screen.

   Input Parameters
   ----------------
   i       - Integer i is written to the screen.
   width  - Maximum, right justified, representation.
             If the representation uses fewer than width
             digits, blanks are added on the left. If the
             representation will not fit in width digits,
             then the width parameter is ignored.
                                                              *)

PROCEDURE writecard
              (       c      : CARDINAL                (* in *);
                      width : CARDINAL                 (* in *) );
(*
   Writes cardinal c to the screen.

   Input Parameters
   ----------------
   c       - Cardinal c is written to the screen.
   width  - Maximum, right justified, representation.
```

```
                    If the representation uses fewer than width
                    digits, blanks are added on the left. If the
                    representation will not fit in width digits,
                    then the width parameter is ignored.
                                                                  *)

PROCEDURE centermessage
                (    s  : ARRAY OF CHAR          (* in *) );
 (*
    Writes the string s centered on the screen.

    Input Parameters
    ----------------
    s - Centers the string s on the screen.  If the string
        is larger than 80 characters, does nothing.
                                                                  *)

PROCEDURE spacebar;
 (*
    Puts the message "Hit spacebar to continue -->" on
    line 24 of the screen.  Program execution pauses until
    a spacebar is hit.
                                                                  *)

PROCEDURE yes() : BOOLEAN;
 (*
    Pauses program execution until one of the characters
    'Y', 'y', 'N', or 'n' is entered from the keyboard.  If
    the entered character is 'Y' or 'y', true is returned
    otherwise false is returned.
                                                                  *)

END termio.
```

**Figure 3.8** Definition module Termio

Figure 3.9 gives the implementation details for this module termio.

Module termio typifies the kind of customization of input and output that is possible in Modula-2. This module will be published by John Wiley and Sons with many other software components in a book entitled, *Modula-2 Software Components* by Richard Sincovec and Richard Wiener.

```
IMPLEMENTATION MODULE termio;

FROM SYSTEM IMPORT
   (* const *) AX, DI, ES, CX, DX, BX,
   (* type  *) ADDRESS,
   (* proc  *) CODE, GETREG, ADR, SETREG, DOSCALL;
```

*(continued)*

```
VAR
   card : CARDINAL; (* 1 if monochrome, 2 if graphics. *)
   mode : modetype; (* normal, reverse, underline, or
                          highlight.                    *)

PROCEDURE clrtoeol;

VAR
    x, y : CARDINAL;

BEGIN
  getxy( x, y );
  repeatwrite( ' ', 79 - x );
  gotoxy( x, y );
END clrtoeol;


PROCEDURE right
          (      x    : CARDINAL                (* in *) );

VAR
    xpos, ypos : CARDINAL;

BEGIN
  getxy( xpos, ypos );
  IF xpos + x <= 79
  THEN
    gotoxy( xpos + x, ypos );
  END(* if then *);
END right;


PROCEDURE left
          (      x    : CARDINAL                (* in *) );

VAR
    xpos, ypos : CARDINAL;

BEGIN
  getxy( xpos, ypos );
  IF x <= xpos
  THEN
    gotoxy ( xpos - x, ypos );
  END(* if then *);
END left;


PROCEDURE up
          (      x    : CARDINAL                (* in *) );

VAR
    xpos, ypos : CARDINAL;

BEGIN
  getxy( xpos, ypos );
  IF x <= ypos
  THEN
    gotoxy( xpos, ypos - x );
  END(* if then *);
END up;
```

```
PROCEDURE down
         (      x    : CARDINAL                    (* in *) );

VAR
    xpos, ypos : CARDINAL;

BEGIN
  getxy( xpos, ypos );
  IF  x  <= 24 - ypos
  THEN
    gotoxy( xpos, ypos + x );
  END(* if then *);
END down;


PROCEDURE clrscreen;

BEGIN
  write( CHR( 12 ) );  (* form feed *)
END clrscreen;


PROCEDURE findchar
         (      ch  : CHAR           (* in *);
                len : CARDINAL       (* in *);
                adr : ADDRESS        (* in *) ) : CARDINAL;
(* Returns the offset position of ch, if present,
   in len bytes starting at address adr.  If ch is
   not present, returns len.  May be used to compute
   the length of a string by calling
   findchar( 0C, len, ADR( s ) ).                        *)

BEGIN
  (* Save the current DI.                        *)
  CODE( 57H );                    (* PUSH DI *)
  (* Save the current ES.                        *)
  CODE( 06H );                    (* PUSH ES *)
  SETREG( ES, adr.SEGMENT );
  SETREG( DI, adr.OFFSET );
  CODE( 57H );                    (* PUSH DI *)
  (* Set direction flag to increment.            *)
  CODE( 0FCH );                   (* CLD      *)
  (* Search for 0H target.                       *)
  (* Set the counter register, CX, to len.       *)
  SETREG( CX, len + 1 );
  (* The loop ends if CX = 0 or a matchup
     to the byte in AL is found.                  *)
  (* Load AL with target 0H.                     *)
  SETREG( AX, ch );
  CODE( 0F2H, 0AEH );       (* REPNE SCASB   *)
  (* Store the end of string addr in AX.        *)
  CODE( 8BH, 0C7H );        (* MOV AX, DI    *)
  (* Restore original address of string.        *)
  CODE( 5FH );              (* POP DI        *)
  (* Compute the string length in AX.           *)
  CODE( 2BH, 0C7H );        (* SUB AX, DI    *)
  CODE( 2DH, 01H, 00H );   (* SUB AX, 1     *)
  (* Restore the original values of ES
     and DI.                                      *)
```

*(continued)*

```
    CODE( 07H );                 (* POP ES       *)
    CODE( 5FH );                 (* POP DI       *)
    GETREG( AX, len );
    RETURN len;
END findchar;


PROCEDURE getvideocard
         ( VAR card : CARDINAL              (* out *) );
(* Returns 1 if monochrome, 2 if graphics card.      *)

VAR
     result : POINTER TO CHAR;

BEGIN
  result := 0H:449H;
  IF ORD( result^ ) = 7
  THEN
    card := 1;
  ELSE
    card := 2;
  END(* if then *);
END getvideocard;


PROCEDURE setmode
         (   m :   modetype                (* in *) );

BEGIN
  mode := m;
END setmode;


PROCEDURE getmode
         ( VAR m   : modetype              (* out *) );

BEGIN
  m := mode;
END getmode;


PROCEDURE getxy
         ( VAR x, y : CARDINAL             (* out *) );
(* Returns the horizontal and vertical (x, y) position
   of the cursor.                                   *)

VAR
     result : CARDINAL;

BEGIN
  CODE( 55H );                 (* PUSH BP       *)
  CODE( 0B8H, 00H, 03H );      (* MOV AX, 300H *)
  CODE( 0BBH, 00H, 00H );      (* MOV BX, 0H   *)
  CODE( 0CDH, 10H );           (* INT 10       *)
  GETREG( DX, result );
  y := result DIV 256;
  x := result - y * 256;
  CODE( 5DH );                 (* POP BP        *)
END getxy;
```

```
PROCEDURE gotoxy
          (    x, y : CARDINAL              (* in *) );
(* Sets the cursor at horizontal position x (0-79),
   vertical position y (0-24).                        *)



VAR
     a : CARDINAL;

BEGIN
  IF ( x >= 0 ) AND ( x <= 79 ) AND ( y >= 0 ) AND
     ( y <= 24 )
  THEN
    IF ( x # 79 ) OR ( y # 24 )
    THEN
       CODE( 55H );                  (* PUSH BP *)
       a := 200H;
       SETREG( AX, a );
       CODE( 50H );                  (* PUSH AX *)
       a := 0H;
       SETREG( BX, a );
       CODE( 53H );                  (* PUSH BX *)
       SETREG( DX, x + 256 * y );
       CODE( 5BH );                  (* POP BX  *)
       CODE( 58H );                  (* POP AX  *)
       CODE( 0CDH, 10H );            (* INT 10  *)
       CODE( 5DH );                  (* POP BP  *)
    END(* if then *);
  END(* if then *);
END gotoxy;


PROCEDURE writestring
          (    s : ARRAY OF CHAR            (* in *) );
(* Writes the character string to the screen with
   normal attribute.                                 *)

VAR
     len  : CARDINAL; (* Length of string *)
     x    : CARDINAL;
     y    : CARDINAL;
     newx : CARDINAL;
     newy : CARDINAL;
     rem  : CARDINAL;
     off  : CARDINAL; (* offset from the beginning of
                         bit-mapped area.            *)

BEGIN
  getxy( x, y );
  off := 160 * y + 2 * x;
  len := findchar( 0C, HIGH( s ) + 1, ADR( s ) );
  IF len < 1
  THEN
    len := 1;
  END(* if then *);
  rem := ( 4000 - off ) DIV 2;
```

*(continued)*

```
          (* Protect from writing beyond the bit-mapped memory
             area.                                            *)
          IF  len > rem
          THEN
            len := rem;
          END(* if then *);
          (* Compute new position of cursor.                  *)
          newx := ( x + len ) MOD 80;
          newy := y + ( x + len ) DIV 80;
          IF newy > 24
          THEN
            newy := 24;
          END(* if then *);
          (* Save current value of the data segment. *)
          CODE( 1EH );              (* PUSH DS         *)
          (* Transfer the stack segment to DS.        *)
          CODE( 8CH, 0D0H );        (* MOV AX, SS      *)
          CODE( 8EH, 0D8H );        (* MOV DS, AX      *)
          (* Save this value of the stack segment     *)
          CODE( 1EH );              (* PUSH DS         *)
          (* Move the current stack offset to SI.     *)
          CODE( 8BH, 0C4H );        (* MOV AX, SP      *)
          CODE( 8BH, 0F0H );        (* MOV SI, AX      *)
          (* Add 4 bytes to SI because of the two
             push operations.                         *)
          CODE( 83H, 0C6H, 04H ); (* ADD SI, 4         *)
          (* Save this value of SI.                    *)
          CODE( 56H );              (* PUSH SI         *)
          (* Transfer the offset to DI.                *)
          SETREG( DI, off );
          (* Get value of SI.                          *)
          CODE( 5EH );              (* POP SI          *)
          (* Starting location of bit mapped memory
             area for monochrome adaptor. Use B800
             for graphics adaptor. Transfer to ES.    *)
          IF card = 1
          THEN
            CODE( 0B8H, 00H, 0B0H );(* MOV AX, B000H *)
          ELSE
            CODE( 0B8H, 00H, 0B8H );(* MOV AX, B800H *)
          END(* if then *);
          CODE( 8EH, 0C0H );          (* MOV ES, AX    *)
          (* Transfer length of string to CX.         *)
          SETREG( CX, len );
          (* Transfer attribute of string to AH.      *)
          IF mode = normal
          THEN
            CODE( 0B4H, 07H );        (* MOV AH, 07H   *)
          ELSIF mode = reverse
          THEN
            CODE( 0B4H, 70H );        (* MOV AH, 70H   *)
          ELSIF mode = highlight
          THEN
            CODE( 0B4H, 0FH );        (* MOV AH, 0FH   *)
          ELSE
            CODE( 0B4H, 1H );         (* MOV AH, 1H    *)
          END(* if then *);
          (* Get value of DS.                         *)
          CODE( 01FH );             (* POP DS          *)
          (* Load byte in DS:DI to AX.                *)
          CODE( 0ACH );             (* TOP : LODSB     *)
          (* Transfer word from AX to ES:DI.          *)
          CODE( 0ABH );             (* STOSW           *)
```

144

```
    (* Continue CX times.                         *)
    CODE( 0E2H, 0FCH );          (* LOOP TOP      *)
    CODE( 01FH );                (* POP DS        *)
    gotoxy( newx, newy );
END writestring;


PROCEDURE inttochar
          (      i   : INTEGER        (* in *) ) : CHAR;

BEGIN
  IF ( i >= 0 ) AND ( i <= 9 )
  THEN
    RETURN CHR( ORD( '0' ) + i );
  ELSE
    RETURN 0C;
  END(* if then *);
END inttochar;


PROCEDURE chartoint
          (      ch  : CHAR          (* in *) ) : INTEGER;

BEGIN
  IF ( ch >= '0' ) AND ( ch <= '9' )
  THEN
    RETURN ORD( ch ) - ORD( '0' );
  ELSE
    RETURN 0;
  END(* if then *);
END chartoint;


PROCEDURE readstring
          ( VAR s   : ARRAY OF CHAR            (* out *) );

VAR
     index : CARDINAL;
     ch    : CHAR;
     temp  : modetype;

BEGIN
  temp := mode;
  mode := normal;
  index := 0;
  read( ch );
  IF ORD( ch ) # bs
  THEN
    write( ch );
  END(* if then *);
  WHILE ch # cr DO
    IF ORD( ch ) = bs
    THEN
      IF index > 0
      THEN
        DEC( index );
        write( ch );
        write( ' ' );
        write( ch );
      END(* if then *);
```

*(continued)*

```
                    ELSE
                      IF index <= HIGH( s )
                      THEN
                        s[ index ] := ch;
                        INC( index );
                      END(* if then *);
                    END(* if then *);
                    read( ch );
                    IF ( ORD( ch ) # bs ) AND ( index <= HIGH( s ) )
                    THEN
                      write( ch );
                    END(* if then *);
                  END(* while *);
                  IF index <= HIGH( s )
                  THEN
                    s[ index ] := OC;
                  END(* if then *);
                  mode := temp;
                END readstring;


  PROCEDURE readint
          ( VAR i    : INTEGER                    (* out *) );

  VAR
        temp    : modetype;
        neg     : BOOLEAN;
        j       : CARDINAL;
        s       : ARRAY[ 0..6 ] OF CHAR;
        err     : BOOLEAN;
        leading : INTEGER;
        ch      : CHAR;
        z       : CARDINAL;

  BEGIN
    temp := mode;
    mode := normal;
    LOOP
      read( ch );
      WHILE ( ( ORD( ch ) < 48 ) OR ( ORD( ch ) > 57 ) ) AND
            ( ch # cr ) AND ( ch # '-' ) DO
        read( ch );
      END(* while *);
      IF ch # cr
      THEN
        write( ch );
      END(* if then *);
      IF ch = cr
      THEN
        i := 0;
        RETURN;
      ELSIF ch = '-'
      THEN
        neg := TRUE;
        j := 0;
      ELSE
        neg := FALSE;
        s[ 0 ] := ch;
        j := 1;
      END(* if then *);
      err := FALSE;
      REPEAT
```

```
read( ch );
IF j = 5
THEN
  WHILE ( ch # cr ) AND ( ORD( ch ) # 8 ) DO
    read( ch );
  END(* while *);
ELSE
  WHILE ( ( ORD( ch ) < 48 ) OR ( ORD( ch ) > 57 ) ) AND
         ( ch # cr ) AND ( ORD( ch ) # 8 ) DO
    read( ch );
  END(* while *);
END(* if then *);
IF ( ORD( ch ) # bs ) AND ( ch # cr )
THEN
  write( ch );
END(* if then *);
IF ORD( ch ) = bs
THEN
  IF j > 0
  THEN
    write( ch );
    write( ' ' );
    write( ch );
    DEC( j );
    IF j = 0
    THEN
      IF neg
      THEN
        write( ch );
        write( ' ' );
        write( ch );
      END(* if then *);
    END(* if then *);
  END(* if then *);
  ELSE
  IF ch # cr
  THEN
    s[ j ] := ch;
    INC( j );
  END(* if then *);
END(* if then *);
UNTIL ( j = 6 ) OR ( ch = cr ) OR ( j = 0 );
IF j # 0
THEN
  s[ j ] := 0C;
  IF s[ 0 ] = 0C
  THEN
    i := 0;
  ELSE
    i := 0;
    j := 0;
    REPEAT
      IF j = 4
      THEN
        leading := chartoint( s[ 0 ] );
        IF leading >= 4
        THEN
          err := TRUE;
        END(* if then *);
        IF leading = 3
        THEN
```

*(continued)*

```
               IF ( ( i = 3276 ) AND
               ( chartoint( s[ 4 ] ) > 7 ) ) OR
               ( i >= 3277 )
               THEN
                  err := TRUE;
               END(* if then *);
          END(* if then *);
       END(* if then *);
       IF NOT err
       THEN
          i := 10 * i + chartoint( s[ j ] );
       END(* if then *);
       INC( j );
     UNTIL ( err ) OR ( s[ j ] = OC ) OR ( j = 5 );
   END(* if then *);
   IF err
   THEN
     IF NOT neg
     THEN
       FOR z := 1 TO j + 1 DO
         write( CHR( 8 ) ); (* backspace *)
       END(* for *);
       FOR z := 1 TO j + 1 DO
         write( ' ' );
       END(* for *);
       FOR z := 1 TO j DO
         write( CHR( 8 ) );
       END(* for *);
          ELSE
            FOR z := 1 TO j + 2 DO
              write( CHR( 8 ) ); (* backspace *)
            END(* for *);
            FOR z := 1 TO j + 2 DO
              write( ' ' );
            END(* for *);
            FOR z := 1 TO j + 1 DO
              write( CHR( 8 ) );
            END(* for *);
          END(* if then *);
        ELSE
          EXIT;
        END(* if then *);
     END(* if then *);
   END(* loop *);
   IF neg
   THEN
     i := -i;
   END(* if then *);
   mode := temp;
END readint;


PROCEDURE readcard
        ( VAR c    : CARDINAL                    (* out *) );

VAR
    ch      : CHAR;
    temp    : modetype;
    i, j    : CARDINAL;
    s       : ARRAY[ 0..6 ] OF CHAR;
    err     : BOOLEAN;
    leading : CARDINAL;
```

```
BEGIN
  temp := mode;
  mode := normal;
  LOOP
    err := FALSE;
    j := 0;
    REPEAT
      read( ch );
      IF j = 5
      THEN
        WHILE ( ch # cr ) AND ( ORD( ch ) # 8 ) DO
          read( ch );
        END(* while *);
      ELSE
        WHILE ( ( ORD( ch ) < 48 ) OR ( ORD( ch ) > 57 ) ) AND
              ( ch # cr ) AND ( ORD( ch ) # 8 ) DO
          read( ch );
        END(* while *);
      END(* if then *);
      IF ( ORD( ch ) # bs ) AND ( ch # cr )
      THEN
        write( ch );
      END(* if then *);
      IF ORD( ch ) = bs
      THEN
        IF j > 0
        THEN
          write( ch );
          write( ' ' );
          write( ch );
          DEC( j );
        END(* if then *);
      ELSE
        IF ch # cr
        THEN
          s[ j ] := ch;
          INC( j );
        END(* if then *);
      END(* if then *);
    UNTIL ( j = 6 ) OR ( ch = cr );
    s[ j ] := OC;
    IF s[ 0 ] = OC
    THEN
      c := 0;
    ELSE
      c := 0;
      j := 0;
      REPEAT
        IF j = 4
        THEN
          leading := CARDINAL( chartoint( s[ 0 ] ) );
          IF leading >= 7
          THEN
            err := TRUE;
          END(* if then *);
          IF leading = 6
          THEN
            IF ( ( c = 6553 ) AND
            ( chartoint( s[ 4 ] ) > 5 ) ) OR
            ( c >= 6554 )
```

*(continued)*

```
            THEN
               err := TRUE;
               END(* if then *);
            END(* if then *);
         END(* if then *);
         IF NOT err
         THEN
            c := 10 * c + CARDINAL( chartoint( s[ j ] ) );
         END(* if then *);
         INC( j );
       UNTIL ( err ) OR ( s[ j ] = 0C ) OR ( j = 5 );
      END(* if then *);
      IF err
      THEN
        FOR i := 1 TO j + 1 DO
          write( CHR( 8 ) ); (* backspace *)
        END(* for *);
        FOR i := 1 TO j + 1 DO
          write( ' ' );
        END(* for *);
        FOR i := 1 TO j DO
          write( CHR( 8 ) );
        END(* for *);
      ELSE
        EXIT;
      END(* if then *);
    END(* loop *);
    mode := temp;
  END readcard;


  PROCEDURE read
          ( VAR ch : CHAR                        (* out *) );

  PROCEDURE convert
            ( VAR ch : CHAR                       (* in *) );

    BEGIN
      CASE ORD(ch) OF
        59: ch := CHR(128) |    71: ch := CHR(167) |
        60: ch := CHR(129) |    72: ch := CHR(161) |
        61: ch := CHR(130) |    73: ch :- CHR(165) |
        62: ch := CHR(131) |    75: ch := CHR(164) |
        63: ch := CHR(132) |    77: ch := CHR(163) |
        64: ch := CHR(133) |    79: ch := CHR(168) |
        65: ch := CHR(134) |    80: ch := CHR(162) |
        66: ch := CHR(135) |    81: ch := CHR(166) |
        67: ch := CHR(136) |    83: ch := CHR(169) |
        68: ch := CHR(137) |    15: ch := CHR(170) |
        82: ch := nul;
           ins := NOT ins
      ELSE
        ch := nul
      END (* case *)
    END convert;

BEGIN (* read *)
  DOSCALL( 8H, ch );
  IF ch = 0C
  THEN
    DOSCALL( 8H, ch );
    convert(ch)
```

```
    ELSE
      CASE ch OF
        1C : ch := CHR(138)| 2C  : ch := CHR(139)|
        3C : ch := CHR(140)| 4C  : ch := CHR(141)|
        5C : ch :=·CHR(142)| 6C  : ch := CHR(143)|
        7C : ch := CHR(144)| 12C: ch := CHR(145)|
        13C: ch := CHR(146)| 14C: ch := CHR(147)|
        16C: ch := CHR(148)| 17C: ch := CHR(149)|
        20C: ch := CHR(150)| 21C: ch := CHR(151)|
        22C: ch := CHR(152)| 23C: ch := CHR(153)|
        24C: ch := CHR(154)| 25C: ch := CHR(155)|
        26C: ch := CHR(156)| 27C: ch := CHR(157)|
        30C: ch := CHR(158)| 31C: ch := CHR(159)|
        32C: ch := CHR(160)| 36C: ch := CHR(171)
      ELSE;  (* do nothing *)
      END(* case *)
  END (* if then *)
END read;


PROCEDURE echoread
          ( VAR ch : CHAR                        (* out *) );

VAR
     temp : modetype;

BEGIN
  temp := mode;
  mode := normal;
  read( ch );
  write( ch );
  mode := temp;
END echoread;


PROCEDURE writecard
          (    c       : CARDINAL              (* in *);
               width : CARDINAL                (* in *) );

VAR
     divisor : CARDINAL;
     j       : CARDINAL;
     digits  : CARDINAL;

BEGIN
  IF c >= 10000
  THEN
    digits := 5;
    divisor := 10000;
  ELSIF c >= 1000
  THEN
    digits := 4;
    divisor := 1000;
  ELSIF c >= 100
  THEN
    digits := 3;
    divisor := 100;
  ELSIF c >= 10
```

*(continued)*

```
          THEN
            digits := 2;
            divisor := 10;
          ELSE
            digits := 1;
          END(* if then *);
          IF width > digits
          THEN
            FOR j := 1 TO width - digits DO
              write( ' ' );
            END(* for *);
          END(* if then *);
          IF c > 9
          THEN
            REPEAT
              j := c DIV divisor;
              write( inttochar( INTEGER( j ) ) );
              DEC( c, j * divisor );
              divisor := divisor DIV 10;
            UNTIL divisor = 1;
            write( inttochar( INTEGER( c ) ) );
          ELSE
            write( inttochar( INTEGER( c ) ) );
          END(* if then *);
        END writecard;


        PROCEDURE writeint
                  (       i     : INTEGER              (* in *);
                        width : CARDINAL               (* in *) );

        VAR
            digits : CARDINAL;
            j      : CARDINAL;

        BEGIN
          IF ABS( i ) >= 10000
          THEN
            digits := 5;
          ELSIF ABS( i ) >= 1000
          THEN
            digits :- 4;
          ELSIF ABS( i ) >= 100
          THEN
            digits := 3;
          ELSIF ABS( i ) >= 10
          THEN
            digits := 2;
          ELSE
            digits := 1;
          END(* if then *);
          IF width > digits
          THEN
            FOR j := 1 TO width - digits DO
              write( ' ' );
            END(* for *);
          END(* if then *);
          IF i < 0
          THEN
            write( '-' );
          END(* if then *);
          writecard( ABS( i ), 1 );
        END writeint;
```

```
PROCEDURE write
        (       ch : CHAR                      (* in *) );

VAR
    s    : ARRAY[ 0..0 ] OF CHAR;
    temp : modetype;

BEGIN(* write *)
  temp := mode;
  IF ( ORD( ch ) <= 32 ) OR ( ORD( ch ) >= 127 )
  THEN
    mode := normal;
    IF ORD( ch ) = bs
    THEN
      DOSCALL (6, 10C); (* Backspace *)
      DOSCALL (6, ' ');
      DOSCALL (6, 10C); (* Backspace *)
    ELSIF ch = 14C
    THEN (* Form feed *)
      DOSCALL (6, 33C);
      DOSCALL (6, '[');
      DOSCALL (6, '2');
      DOSCALL (6, 'J');
    ELSE
      DOSCALL (6, ch);
    END(* if then *);
  ELSE
    s[ 0 ] := ch;
    writestring( s );
  END(* if then *);
  mode := temp;
END write;


PROCEDURE repeatwrite
        (       ch     : CHAR              (* in *);
                numrep : CARDINAL          (* in *) );

VAR
    s    : ARRAY[ 0..1999 ] OF CHAR;
    i    : CARDINAL;
    x, y : CARDINAL;

BEGIN
  getxy( x, y );
  IF numrep < 2000 - 80 * y + 2 * x
  THEN
    FOR i := 0 TO numrep - 1 DO
      s[ i ] := ch;
    END(* for *);
    s[ numrep ] := 0C;
    writestring( s );
  END(* if then *);
END repeatwrite;


PROCEDURE writeln;

VAR
    temp : modetype;
```

*(continued)*

```
BEGIN
  temp := mode;
  mode := normal;
  write( CHR( 13 ) );
  write( CHR( 10 ) );
  mode := temp;
END writeln;


PROCEDURE centermessage
          (     s   : ARRAY OF CHAR           (* in *) );

VAR
     i   : CARDINAL;
     len : CARDINAL;

BEGIN
  IF HIGH( s ) <= 79
  THEN
    i := 0;
    WHILE ( i <= HIGH( s ) ) AND ( s[ i ] # 0C ) DO
      INC( i );
    END(* while *);
    len := i;
    right( 40 - len DIV 2 );
    writestring( s );
  END(* if then *);
END centermessage;


PROCEDURE spacebar;

VAR
     ch : CHAR;

BEGIN
  getmode( mode );
  setmode( normal );
  gotoxy( 0,  24  );
  centermessage( "Hit spacebar to continue -->" );
  read( ch );
  WHILE ( ch # bkch ) DO
    read( ch );
  END(* while *);
  setmode( mode );
END spacebar;


PROCEDURE yes() : BOOLEAN;

VAR
     ch : CHAR;

BEGIN
  getmode( mode );
  setmode( normal );
  REPEAT
    read( ch );
  UNTIL ( ch = 'y' ) OR ( ch = 'Y' ) OR ( ch = 'N' )
        OR ( ch = 'n' );
```

```
    write(  ch  );
    setmode( mode );
    RETURN ( ch = 'y' ) OR ( ch = 'Y' );
  END yes;

BEGIN
  mode := normal;
  getvideocard( card );
END termio.
```

**Figure 3.9** Implementation module Termio

# Other Modula-2 Libraries

- **Standard Modula-2 Libraries**

# Standard Modula-2 Libraries

This section lists other important Modula-2 libraries.

As we discussed in Section 3, standardization of a Modula-2 library may be as important as the standardization of the language. A standard library environment will allow programs to be transported across different machines, across operating systems, and across directory structures.

The new standard Modula-2 libraries presented in this section have been provided in beta test form to the author by Logitech, Inc., Veterans Boulevard, Redwood City, Ca. 94063. They are reproduced with permission from Logitech, Inc. Although some of the details may have changed slightly by the time this book is published, it is expected that the current version is close to final. The reader is encouraged to check with Logitech or MODUS for the latest details.

Each library is presented in a separate figure. The comments throughout are given by Logitech.

```
DEFINITION MODULE ASCII;
(* Symbolic constants for non-printing ASCII characters.
   This module has an empty implementation.            *)

EXPORT QUALIFIED
    (* const *) nul, soh, stx, etx, eot, enq, ack, bel, bs,
                ht,  lf,  vt,  ff,  cr,  so,  si, dle, dc1,
                dc2, dc3, dc4, nak, syn, etb, can, em,  sub,
                esc, fs,  gs,  rs,  us, del, EOL;

  CONST
      nul = 00C; soh = 01C; stx = 02C; etx = 03C;
      eot = 04C; enq = 05C; ack = 06C; bel = 07C;
      bs  = 10C; ht  = 11C; lf  = 12C; vt  = 13C;
      ff  = 14C; cr  = 15C; so  = 16C; si  = 17C;
      dle = 20C; dc1 = 21C; dc2 = 22C; dc3 = 23C;
      dc4 = 24C; nak = 25C; syn = 26C; etb = 27C;
      can = 30C; em  = 31C; sub = 32C; esc = 33C;
      fs  = 34C; gs  = 35C; rs  = 36C; us  = 37C;
      del = 177C, EOL = 36C;

END ASCII.
```

**Figure 4.1** Standard module ASCII

```
DEFINITION MODULE Binary;

  FROM Files IMPORT File, FileState;

  FROM SYSTEMToBeImpl IMPORT BYTECOUNT;

  FROM SYSTEM IMPORT BYTE, WORD, ADDRESS;

  EXPORT QUALIFIED
    (* proc *) ReadByte, ReadWord, ReadBlock, ReadBytes,
               WriteByte, WriteWord, WriteBlock, WriteBytes;
```

```
    PROCEDURE ReadByte (     file      : File;
                         VAR byte      : BYTE;
                         VAR state     : FileState);
    (* Read one byte from a binary file.                    *)

    PROCEDURE ReadWord (     file      : File;
                         VAR word      : WORD;
                         VAR state     : FileState);
    (* Read one word from a binary file.                    *)

    PROCEDURE ReadBlock(file           : File;
                         VAR block     : ARRAY OF BYTE;
                         VAR state     : FileState);
    (* Read an arbitrary variable from a binary file.       *)

    PROCEDURE ReadBytes(     file      : File;
                             addr      : ADDRESS;
                             bytes     : BYTECOUNT;
                         VAR bytesRead : BYTECOUNT;
                         VAR state     : FileState);
    (* Read an arbitrary number of bytes from a binary file.
       Initial byte can NOT be written to any byte within a
       word on word addressed machines.                     *)


    PROCEDURE WriteByte(     file      : File;
                             byte      : BYTE;
                         VAR state     : FileState);
    (* Write one byte to a binary file.                     *)

    PROCEDURE WriteWord(     file      : File;
                             word      : WORD;
                         VAR state     : FileState);
    (* Write one word to a binary file.                     *)

    PROCEDURE WriteBlock (   file      : File;
                         block         : ARRAY OF BYTE;
                         VAR state     : FileState);
    (* Write an arbitrary variable to a binary file.        *)

    PROCEDURE WriteBytes (   file      : File;
                             addr      : ADDRESS;
                             bytes     : BYTECOUNT;
                         VAR state     : FileState);
    (* Write an arbitrary number of bytes to a binary file.
       Initial byte can NOT come from any byte within a word
       on word addressed machines.                          *)

END Binary.
```

**Figure 4.2** Standard module Binary

```
DEFINITION MODULE Convert;

  FROM SYSTEM IMPORT WORD;

  EXPORT QUALIFIED
    (* proc *) IntToStr, StrToInt, CardToStr, StrToCard,
               NumToStr, StrToNum;
```

*(continued)*

```
PROCEDURE IntToStr (     int     : INTEGER;
                     VAR str     : ARRAY OF CHAR;
                         width   : CARDINAL;
                     VAR success : BOOLEAN);

PROCEDURE CardToStr(     card    : CARDINAL;
                     VAR str     : ARRAY OF CHAR;
                         width   : CARDINAL;
                     VAR success : BOOLEAN);

PROCEDURE NumToStr  (     num     : WORD;
                     VAR str     : ARRAY OF CHAR;
                         base    : CARDINAL (* [2..36] *);
                         width   : CARDINAL;
                     VAR success : BOOLEAN);

PROCEDURE StrToInt (     str     : ARRAY OF CHAR;
                     VAR int     : INTEGER;
                     VAR success : BOOLEAN);

PROCEDURE StrToCard(     str     : ARRAY OF CHAR;
                     VAR card    : CARDINAL;
                     VAR success : BOOLEAN);

PROCEDURE StrToNum (     str     : ARRAY OF CHAR;
                     VAR num     : WORD;
                         base    : CARDINAL (* [2..36] *);
                     VAR success : BOOLEAN);
```

END Convert.

**Figure 4.3** Standard module Convert

```
DEFINITION MODULE ConvertReal;

  EXPORT QUALIFIED
    (* proc *) RealToStr, StrToReal;

  PROCEDURE RealToStr (     real     : REAL;
                        VAR str      : ARRAY OF CHAR;
                            width    : CARDINAL;
                            decPlaces : INTEGER;
                        (* neg -> sci; 0 -> no point *)
                        VAR success  : BOOLEAN);

  PROCEDURE StrToReal (     str      : ARRAY OF CHAR;
                        VAR real     : REAL;
                        VAR success  : BOOLEAN);
```

END ConvertReal.

**Figure 4.4** Standard module ConvertReal

```
DEFINITION MODULE Directory;

  FROM Files IMPORT FileState;

  EXPORT QUALIFIED
    (* type *) FileNameType, DirQueryProc,
    (* proc *) Rename, Delete, DirQuery, TypeOfFileName;
```

```
TYPE
    FileNameType = (invalidName, singleName, wildName);
    DirQueryProc = PROCEDURE (ARRAY OF CHAR, VAR BOOLEAN);

PROCEDURE Rename     (    fromName : ARRAY OF CHAR;
                          toName   : ARRAY OF CHAR;
                      VAR state    : FileState);

PROCEDURE Delete     (    fileName : ARRAY OF CHAR;
                      VAR state    : FileState);

PROCEDURE TypeOfFileName(name      : ARRAY OF CHAR)
                                   : FileNameType;

PROCEDURE DirQuery (     wildCard : ARRAY OF CHAR;
                         dirProc  : DirQueryProc;
                     VAR state    : FileState);
(* DirQuery is passed a unique or wild-card file name
   (implementation dependent) and repeatedly calls
   DirProc to process each file name which meets the
   wild-card specification.  DirQuery stops calling
   DirProc whenever DirProc returns FALSE (DirProc
   returns a "keep going" value).                      *)

END Directory.
```

**Figure 4.5** Standard module Directory

```
DEFINITION MODULE FilePositions;
(* May be used for Text or Binary files, but mixed mode
   usage is very non-portable.                          *)

  FROM Files IMPORT File, FileState;

  FROM SYSTEMToBeImpl IMPORT ADDRESSINC;

  IMPORT OSFileInfo;

  EXPORT QUALIFIED
    (* type *) FilePosition,
    (* proc *) GetFilePos, SetFilePos, CalcFilePos, GetEOF,
               GetBOF;

  TYPE
      FilePosition = OSFileInfo.FilePosition;

(* WARNING!   THIS IS NOT OPAQUE, BUT SHOULD BE TREATED
             AS SUCH.
   Its contents are implementation-dependent, and should
   not be manipulated directly.  It is implemented as a
   RECORD, not a POINTER, so its contents may be written
   to/from files. It SHOULD be an opaque type, but this
   compromise was made so that its contents could be
   recorded in files.                                   *)


  PROCEDURE GetFilePos     (    file      : File;
                            VAR pos       : FilePosition);
  (* Returns the current position in the file.          *)
```

*(continued)*

```
PROCEDURE GetEOF  (          file          : File;
                       VAR pos              : FilePosition);
(* Returns a FilePosition of the current end of the
   file.                                            *)

PROCEDURE GetBOF  (          file          : File;
                       VAR pos              : FilePosition);
(* Returns a FilePosition of the beginning of the file. *)

PROCEDURE CalcFilePos (      file          : File;
                       VAR pos              : FilePosition;
                           numOfElements : INTEGER;
                           elementLength : ADDRESSINC);
(* Calculate a file·position relative to FilePos, offset
   by NumOfElements. Return the resulting position in
   FilePos.                                          *)
(* Note: A program which calls this procedure passing a
   file which was Opened/Created as textMode is probably
   not portable.                                     *)

PROCEDURE SetFilePos    (    file          : File;
                             pos           : FilePosition;
                       VAR state          : FileState);
(* Positions the file as specified.  Illegal position
   leaves the file as it was before the call and returns
   a bad state.                                      *)

END FilePositions.
```

**Figure 4.6** Standard module FilePositions

```
DEFINITION MODULE MathLib;

   EXPORT QUALIFIED
     (* proc *) Sqrt, Exp, Ln, Sin, Cos, Arctan, Entier,
                Power;

   PROCEDURE Sqrt   (real : REAL) : REAL;

   PROCEDURE Exp    (real : REAL) : REAL;

   PROCEDURE Ln     (real : REAL) : REAL;

   PROCEDURE Sin    (real : REAL) : REAL;        (* radians *)

   PROCEDURE Cos    (real : REAL) : REAL;

   PROCEDURE Arctan (real : REAL) : REAL;

   PROCEDURE Entier (real : REAL) : INTEGER;
   (* Trunc toward neg inf.                             *)

   PROCEDURE Power  (real : REAL;
                     exp  : REAL) : REAL;
   (* Real to the power exp.                            *)

END MathLib.
```

**Figure 4.7** Standard module MathLib

```
DEFINITION MODULE NumberIO;

  FROM Files IMPORT File, FileState;

  FROM SYSTEM IMPORT WORD;

  EXPORT QUALIFIED
    (* proc *) ReadInt, ReadCard, ReadNum, WriteInt,
               WriteCard, WriteNum;

  PROCEDURE ReadInt (       file    : File;
                        VAR int     : INTEGER;
                        VAR success : BOOLEAN;
                        VAR state   : FileState);

  PROCEDURE ReadCard (      file    : File;
                        VAR card    : CARDINAL;
                        VAR success : BOOLEAN;
                        VAR state   : FileState);

  PROCEDURE ReadNum   (     file    : File;
                        VAR num     : WORD;
                            base    : CARDINAL  (* [2..36] *);
                        VAR success : BOOLEAN;
                        VAR state   : FileState);

  PROCEDURE WriteInt (      file    : File;
                            int     : INTEGER;
                            width   : CARDINAL;
                        VAR state   : FileState);

  PROCEDURE WriteCard (     file    : File;
                            card    : CARDINAL;
                            width   : CARDINAL;
                        VAR state   : FileState);

  PROCEDURE WriteNum (      file    : File;
                            num     : WORD;
                            base    : CARDINAL (* [2..36] *);
                            width   : CARDINAL;
                        VAR state   : FileState);

END NumberIO.
```

**Figure 4.8** Standard module NumberIO

```
DEFINITION MODULE Program;

  EXPORT QUALIFIED
    (* type *) CallResult,
    (* proc *) Call, Terminate, SetInitialization,
               SetTermination;

  TYPE
      CallResult = (  normalReturn,
                      programHalt,
                      keyboardHalt,
```

*(continued)*

```
                                missingProgram,
                                missingModule,
                                duplicateModule,
                                versionError,
                                codeError,
                                programCheck,
                                ioError,
                                otherError );

    PROCEDURE Call(     programName : ARRAY OF CHAR;
                    VAR callResult  : CallResult    );

    PROCEDURE Terminate( reason       : CallResult);

    PROCEDURE SetInitialization( initProc  : PROC);

    PROCEDURE SetTermination( termProc  : PROC);

END Program.
```

**Figure 4.9** Standard module Program

```
DEFINITION MODULE RealIO;

  EXPORT QUALIFIED
    (* proc *) ReadReal, WriteReal;

  PROCEDURE ReadReal  (    VAR real       : REAL;
                           VAR success    : BOOLEAN);

  PROCEDURE WriteReal (        real       : REAL;
                               width       : CARDINAL;
                               decPlaces : INTEGER);

END RealIO.
```

**Figure 4.10** Standard module RealIO

```
 DEFINITION MODULE Storage;

   FROM SYSTEM IMPORT ADDRESS;

   FROM SYSTEMToBeImpl IMPORT ADDRESSINC;

   EXPORT QUALIFIED
     (* proc *) ALLOCATE, DEALLOCATE, CondAllocate;

   PROCEDURE ALLOCATE( VAR ptr     : ADDRESS;
                           size     : ADDRESSINC);

   PROCEDURE DEALLOCATE( VAR ptr     : ADDRESS;
                             size     : ADDRESSINC);

   PROCEDURE CondAllocate( VAR ptr     : ADDRESS;
                               size     : ADDRESSINC;
                           VAR success : BOOLEAN);
 END Storage.
```

**Figure 4.11** Standard module Storage

```
DEFINITION MODULE String;

  EXPORT QUALIFIED
    (* type *) CompareResult,
    (* proc *) Length, Assign, Insert, Delete, Position,
               Substring, Compare, Concat;

  TYPE
      CompareResult = (less, equal, greater);


  PROCEDURE Length(     str        : ARRAY OF CHAR)
                                   : CARDINAL;

  PROCEDURE Assign(     source     : ARRAY OF CHAR;
                    VAR dest       : ARRAY OF CHAR;
                    VAR success    : BOOLEAN);

  PROCEDURE Insert(     source     : ARRAY OF CHAR;
                    VAR dest       : ARRAY OF CHAR;
                        index      : CARDINAL;
                    VAR success    : BOOLEAN);

  PROCEDURE Delete(VAR str         : ARRAY OF CHAR;
                       index       : CARDINAL;
                       len         : CARDINAL;
                   VAR success     : BOOLEAN);

  PROCEDURE Position(    pattern    : ARRAY OF CHAR,
                         source     : ARRAY OF CHAR;
                     VAR index      : CARDINAL;
                     VAR found      : BOOLEAN);

  PROCEDURE Substring(   source     : ARRAY OF CHAR;
                         index      : CARDINAL;
                         len        : CARDINAL;
                     VAR dest       : ARRAY OF CHAR;
                     VAR success    : BOOLEAN);

  PROCEDURE Concat(     source1    : ARRAY OF CHAR;
                        source2    : ARRAY OF CHAR;
                    VAR dest       : ARRAY OF CHAR;
                    VAR success    : BOOLEAN);

  PROCEDURE Compare(    string1    : ARRAY OF CHAR;
                        string2    : ARRAY OF CHAR)
                                   : CompareResult;

END String.
```

**Figure 4.12** Standard module String

```
      DEFINITION MODULE SYSTEMToBeImpl;

        FROM SYSTEM IMPORT WORD;

        EXPORT QUALIFIED
          (* type *) BYTE, ADDRESSINC, BYTECOUNT;
```

*(continued)*

```
TYPE
    BYTE         = WORD;
    ADDRESSINC   = CARDINAL;
    BYTECOUNT    = CARDINAL;

END SYSTEMToBeImpl.
```

**Figure 4.13**  Standard module SYSTEMoBeImp1

SECTION
5

# Recent Changes to Modula-2 and The Borland Modula-2 Implementation

- **Recent Changes in Modula-2**
- **The Borland Turbo Modula-2**

## Recent Changes in Modula-2

In 1985, with the publication of the third edition of *Programming in Modula-2* (Springer-Verlag), Dr. Niklaus Wirth has made some modifications to Modula-2. Most of these changes are minor and involve fine points. There is one major change: the EXPORT QUALIFIED has been removed from definition modules.

Borland International is expected to release both a CP/M and MS-DOS version of Modula-2 in 1986. The recent changes made by Dr. Wirth will be implemented in Turbo Modula-2. It is expected that future versions of the Logitech Modula-2 system and those of other vendors will also adopt these changes.

Figure 5.1 presents, in general terms, a list of changes made by Dr. Wirth. An asterisk next to a listed change implies a major change. A more detailed account of some of these changes is given later in this section.

```
1.   Constant expressions have been extended to general
     expressions with constant operands.

2.   Long integers and long reals (LONGINT and LONGREAL) are
     specified as standard identifiers.

3.   A type specification for subrange types may be used.

4.   Small change in the syntax of a variant record that does
     not contain a variant field.  Empty variants are
     allowed.

5.   A string of length 1 is compatible with the type CHAR.

6.   Empty cases in CASE-statements are allowed.

7.   The starting value and limit of a FOR loop must be
     compatible with the control variable.

8.   The standard procedures MAX and MIN are introduced.

9.   The procedure function TSIZE is no longer restricted to
     returning a CARDINAL value.

10.  The type PROCESS is eliminated from MODULE SYSTEM and is
     replaced by ADDRESS.

*11. The EXPORT QUALIFIED has been eliminated from definition
     modules.
```

**Figure 5.1** Changes to Modula-2

## The Borland Turbo Modula-2

Borland International, the producer of Turbo Pascal, has produced Turbo Modula-2 for the CP/M and MS-DOS environments. They are expected to release these Modula-2 systems in 1986.

Borland is the first major Modula-2 vendor to implement many of the recent changes given in Figure 5.1. In addition to implementing recent changes, these systems provide powerful extensions to the language.

The discussion of Turbo Pascal in this section is based on an evaluation of Borland's CP/M Modula-2 system. It is expected that their MS DOS version will include the same features.

Their compiler provides a compile switch option that allows a programmer to turn off or turn on the extensions. One of the significant extensions that Borland provides in Turbo Modula-2 is Ada-like exception handling. This powerful facility is described and illustrated in this section.

Extended Backus Naur Formalism (EBNF) is used in describing a few of the syntax changes made in Turbo Modula-2.

Figure 5.2 provides a list of changes and extensions that are provided in Turbo Modula-2.

1.  Pascal-like READ, READLN, WRITE, WRITELN procedures are part of the Turbo Modula-2 language and do not have to be imported from an InOut module. Like their Pascal counterparts, these I/O procedures may take a variable number of parameters, each of a different type.

2.  Assignment and comparison operations on strings are allowed. A string is defined as an array of characters, indexed from 0 up to 255 and terminated with the null character, 0C. A string variable may be assigned a string value of a different length. This is in contrast to standard Modula-2 in which aggregate array assignments may only be performed on two arrays that are of assignment compatible type. In standard Modula-2, relational comparisons on strings or any array types are forbidden.

3.  Types LONGINT and LONGREAL are supported and denote standard types. A Turbo Modula-2 LONGREAL literal must be written in scientific notation with a D in front of its exponent (e.g, 0.00D0, 2.68D0, 1.45D-2, 1.78D24). A long integer literal is terminated with an uppercase or lowercase L (e.g. 123456L).

4.  Set elements are not restricted to constants. Expressions may be substituted for ConstExpression in set constructors.

5.  The character tilde, ~, is a synonym for NOT.

6.  The type ADDRESS is compatible with all pointer types and with either CARDINAL or LONGCARD. The interpretation of addresses as numbers is implementation dependent.

*(continued)*

7.  The standard functions MIN and MAX take any scalar type including REAL as an argument and return the types minimum and maximum value, respectively (e.g. MAX( INTEGER) = 32767).

8.  Five standard functions for type conversion are provided. Each of these functions accept arguments of type INTEGER, CARDINAL, LONGINT and REAL. The five functions are:

```
INT    - converts its argument to type INTEGER
CARD   - converts its argument to type CARDINAL
LONG   - converts its argument to type LONGINT
FLOAT  - converts its argument to type REAL
DOUBLE - converts its argument to type LONGREAL
```

9.  All objects declared in a definition module are exported. The explicit export list is discarded. Furthermore, all procedures imported by the definition module are automatically imported into the implementation module. The Turbo Modula-2 compiler does not ignore existing EXPORT lists that may be present from older programs but flags such lists as syntax errors. They must be removed or commented out.

10. The syntax of a variant record type declaration with missing tag field is changed from

```
FieldList = | CASE [ident ":"] qualident OF ...
to
FieldList = | CASE [ident] ":" qualident OF ...
```

11. The syntax of the case statement and the variant record declaration is changed from

```
case    = CaseLabelList ":" StatementSequence
variant = CaseLabelList ":" FieldListSequence
to
case    = [CaseLabelList ":" StatementSequence]
variant = [CaseLabelList ":" FieldListSequence]
```

The inclusion of the empty case and the empty variant allows the insertion of superfluous bars.

12. A string of length 1 is assignment compatible with the type CHAR.

13. The syntax of the subrange type is changed from

```
SubrangeType = "["ConstExpression ".." ConstExpression"]"
to
SubrangeType = [qualident]
               "["ConstExpression ".." ConstExpression "]".
(e.g. i : INTEGER[ 0..9 ]; )
```

14. The type of a formal VAR parameter must be identical, not merely compatible, with its actual parameter. This rule is relaxed for formal parameters of type ADDRESS which are compatible with all pointer types.

15. The types specifying the starting and ending values of the control variable in a FOR loop must be compatible, not merely assignment compatible, with the type of the control variable.

16. The standard identifiers EXCEPTION and RAISE are added to Turbo Modula-2. This far-reaching and significant extension will be discussed and illustrated below.

**Figure 5.2** Changes and extensions in Turbo Modula-2

In Figure 5.3, we illustrate Turbo Modula-2's Pascal-like WRITELN statement.

```
WRITELN( "The integer = ", i, "  The real = ", r,
         "  The character = ", ch, "The string = ", str );
```

**Figure 5.3** Turbo Modula-2's WRITELN

It is expected that the Turbo WRITELN extension will be a boon to the beginning Modula-2 programmer who does not wish to import external modules in his or her early programs.

In Figure 5.4, a segment of code that illustrates long integers is given.

```
VAR
    long1,
    long2,
    long3 : LONGINT;

BEGIN
  long1 := 12345L;
  long2 := 2L;
  long3 := long1 * long2;
  WRITELN( "The long integer product of 12345 x 2 = ",
           long3 );
  WRITELN();
  long3 := long1 DIV long2;
  WRITELN( "The long integer quotient of 12345 and 2 = ",
           long3 );
  long3 := long1 * long1;
  WRITELN( "The long integer product of 12345 * itself = ",
           long3 );
  WRITELN();
  ...
```

**Figure 5.4** Illustration of long integers

Figure 5.5 is a segment of code that shows non-standard Turbo Modula-2 string comparisons.

```
VAR
    s1 : ARRAY[ 0..9 ] OF CHAR;
    s2 : ARRAY[ 0..14 ] OF CHAR;

BEGIN
  s1 := "ABCDE";
  s2 := "ABCEE";
  IF s1 < s2
  THEN
    WRITELN( "s1 < s2" );
  ELSE
    WRITELN( "s1 > s2" );
  END(* if then *);
  WRITELN(); WRITELN();
  . . .
```

**Figure 5.5**  String comparisons in Turbo Modula-2

## Exception Handling in Turbo Modula-2

The most substantial extension provided in Turbo Modula-2 is exception-handling. Exception-handling is particularly important in embedded real-time applications where failure to error-protect a system properly could cause disastrous results.

An exception may be declared anywhere a type declaration can be made, such as

```
TYPE
    EXCEPTION identifier1, identifier2, ..., ;
```

As an example, we may declare the following three exceptions:

```
EXCEPTION rangeerror, dividebyzero, stackoverflow;
```

Associated with every declared exception are one or more exception handlers. An exception handler is activated by a RAISE statement. For example, RAISE rangeerror, or RAISE dividebyzero, or RAISE stackoverflow.

When a RAISE statement is executed, the program searches its procedure call chain for the first handler with the name of the exception that is called in the RAISE statement. If no such handler can be found, the program is terminated.

Exception handlers are blocks of code that must be placed at the very end of a procedure or program, and they begin with the keyword EXCEPTION. Each exception is listed in a manner identical to the labels in a CASE statement.

## *Software Engineering:*

In standard Modula-2 and Pascal, error handling in procedures is typically performed by including an error flag (Boolean parameter) in the procedure. After each call to such a procedure, the value of the error flag must be checked and appropriate action taken if an error has occurred. This approach suffers from two basic shortcomings. The first is that we may not be able to tolerate the erroneous procedure ending before we detect the error. The second is that our code gets littered with many test statements (one after each procedure call).

In Turbo Modula-2, as in Ada, when an exception is raised, control is transferred to an exception handler and then transferred out of the procedure that contains the exception. The program searches for an appropriate exception handler by moving backwards through its procedure call chain.

Figure 5.6 lists a complete Turbo Modula-2 program that contains two exceptions and one handler.

```
MODULE exceptionhandler;
(* This program illustrates exception handling.          *)

   EXCEPTION dividebyzero, overflow;

   PROCEDURE compute
            ( r1, r2 : REAL (* in *) ) : REAL;

   BEGIN
     IF r2 = 0.0
     THEN
       RAISE dividebyzero;
     END(* if then *);
     RETURN r1 / r2;
   END compute;


   PROCEDURE convert
            ( card : CARDINAL (* in *) ) : INTEGER;
```

*(continued)*

```
BEGIN
  IF card > 32767
  THEN
    RAISE overflow;
  END(* if then *);
  RETURN INTEGER( card );
END convert;


VAR
    real1, real2 : REAL;
    quotient     : REAL;
    c            : CARDINAL;
    i            : INTEGER;
BEGIN
  WRITE( "Enter real1 : " );
  READLN( real1 ); WRITELN();
  WRITE( "Enter real2 : " );
  READLN( real2 ); WRITELN();
  quotient := compute( real1, real2 );
  WRITELN(); WRITELN();
  WRITELN( "The quotient = ", quotient );
  WRITELN(); WRITELN();
  WRITE( "Enter a cardinal : " );
  READLN( c );
  WRITELN( "The artificial conversion of the cardinal = ",
           convert( c ) );
  EXCEPTION
    dividebyzero :
      WRITELN(); WRITELN();
      WRITELN( "Divide by zero exception" );
      real2 := 1.0E-30;
      quotient := compute( real1, real2 );
      WRITELN(); WRITELN();
      WRITELN( "The quotient = ", quotient );      |
    overflow :
      c := 32767;
      WRITELN( convert( c ) );
END exceptionhandler;
```

**Figure 5.6** Turbo Modula exception handler

Figure 5.7 illustrates exception propagation. This example was originally written in Ada, in the book *Programming in ADA* by Wiener and Sincovec. It works just as well in Turbo Modula-2.

When procedure one first raises the exception trouble, this exception is handled in procedure two, because of the call chain. The string

Exception handler in procedure two

is displayed on the screen. Procedure two is terminated after this exception is raised and the statement

    x := 2.0 * x

is never executed. The main program calls one ( x ). The value of x was set to 1.0 in the exception handler of procedure two. Thus, procedure one again raises the exception trouble. This time, the exception is handled in the main program because of the call chain. The string

Exception handler in main program

is displayed on the screen.

Figure 5.7 illustrates the fact that exception handlers may be strategically placed at the end of subprogram blocks anywhere in a program to achieve a desired result.

```
MODULE exceptionpropagation;
(* This program illustrates exception propagation.        *)

  EXCEPTION trouble;

  VAR
      x : REAL;

  PROCEDURE one
          ( VAR x : REAL (* in/out *) );

  BEGIN
    x := x - 1.0;
    IF x = 0.0
    THEN
      RAISE trouble;
    END(* if then *);
  END one;

  PROCEDURE two
          ( VAR x : REAL (* in/out *) );

  BEGIN
    x := x + 1.0;
    one( x );
    x := 2.0 * x;
    EXCEPTION
      trouble :
        WRITELN( "Exception handler in procedure two. " );
        x := 1.0;
  END two;
```

*(continued)*

```
BEGIN
  x  := 0.0;
  two( x );
  one( x );
  WRITELN( "x = ", x );
  EXCEPTION
    trouble :
      WRITELN( "Exception handler in main program. " );
END exceptionpropagation.
```

**Figure 5.7** Exception propagation

# Appendixes

- **Syntax of Modula-2**
- **Modula-2 Reserved Words, Operators, Delimiters, and Predefined Procedures**
- **ASCII Character Set**
- **References and Resources**

# Syntax of Modula-2

This appendix is taken with permission from *Modula-2: A Software Development Approach* by Ford and Wiener, John Wiley & Sons (1986) and presents the collected syntax charts for Modula-2.

compilation unit

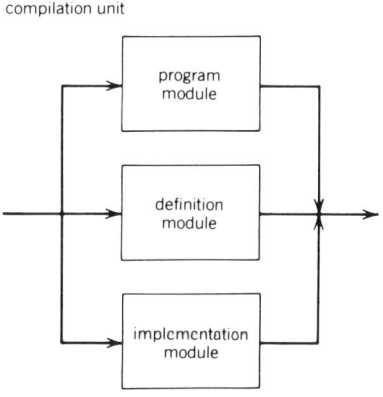

program module

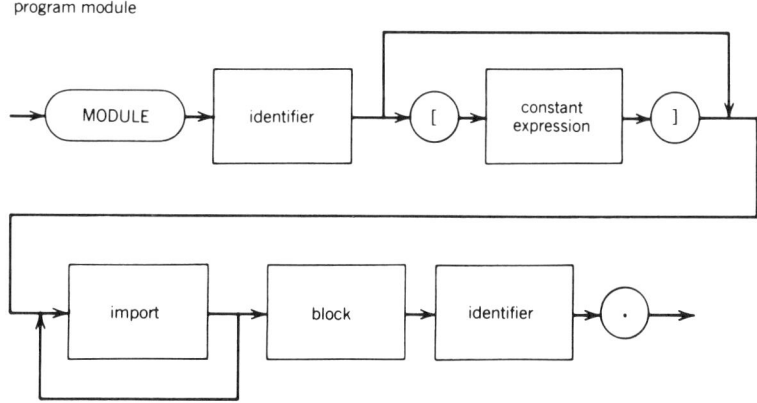

definition module

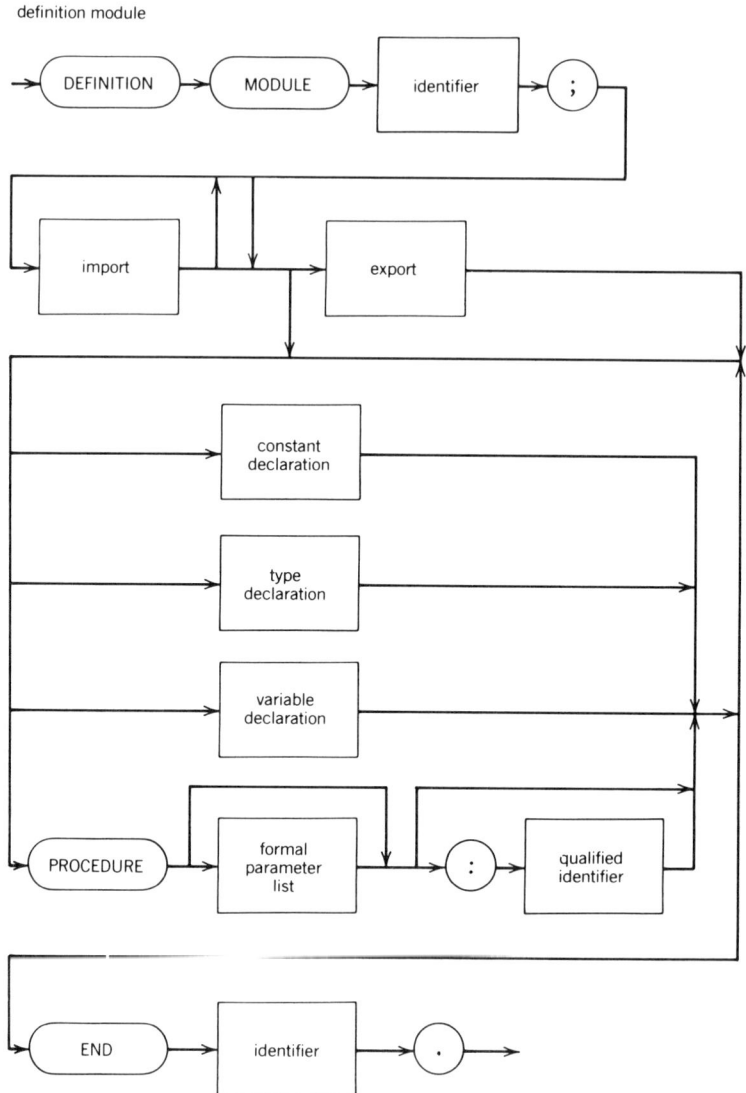

implementation module

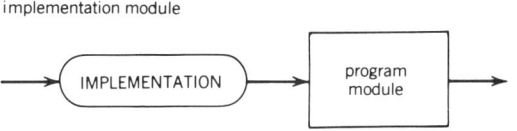

import

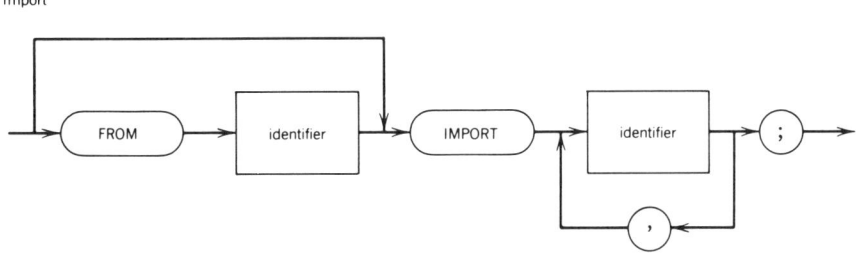

export

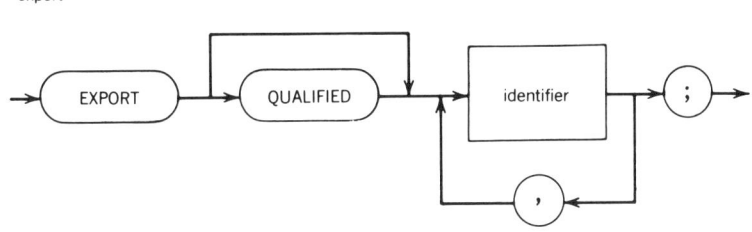

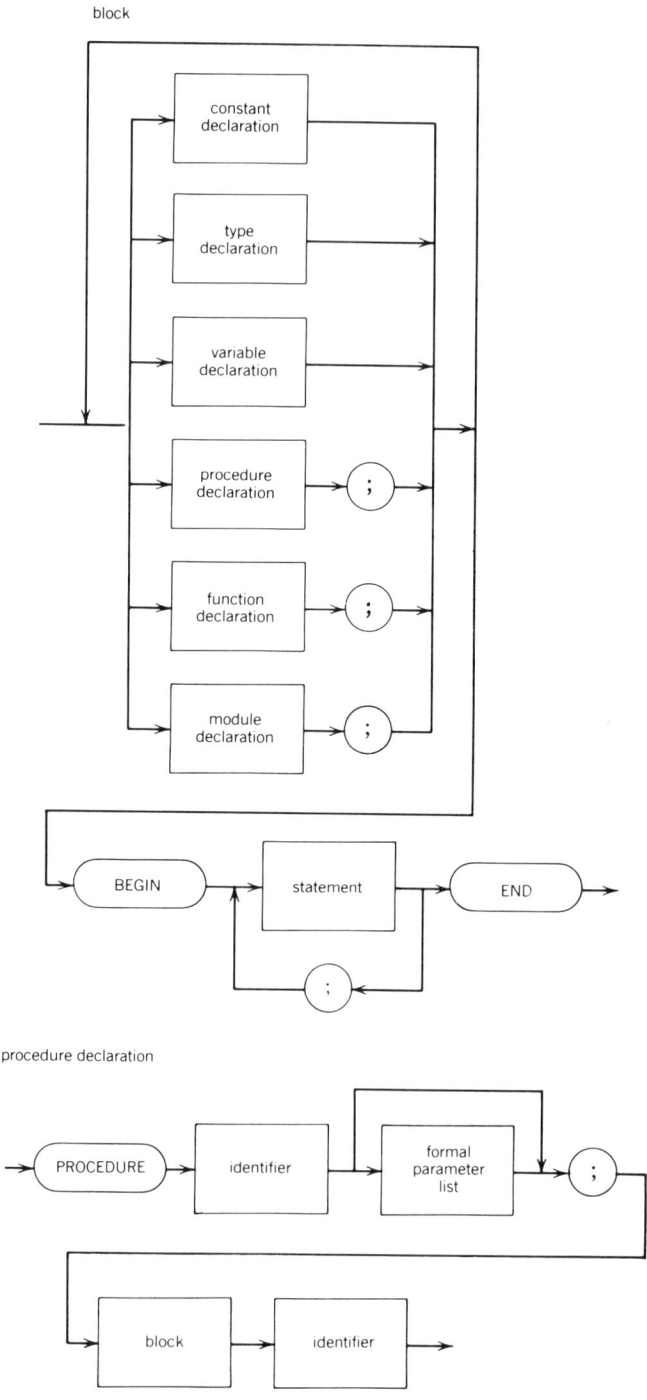

block

procedure declaration

function declaration

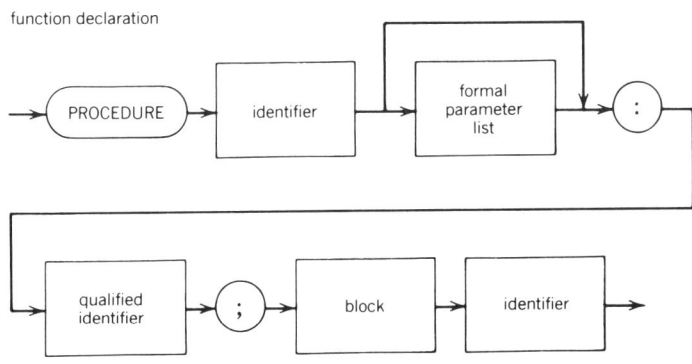

formal parameter list

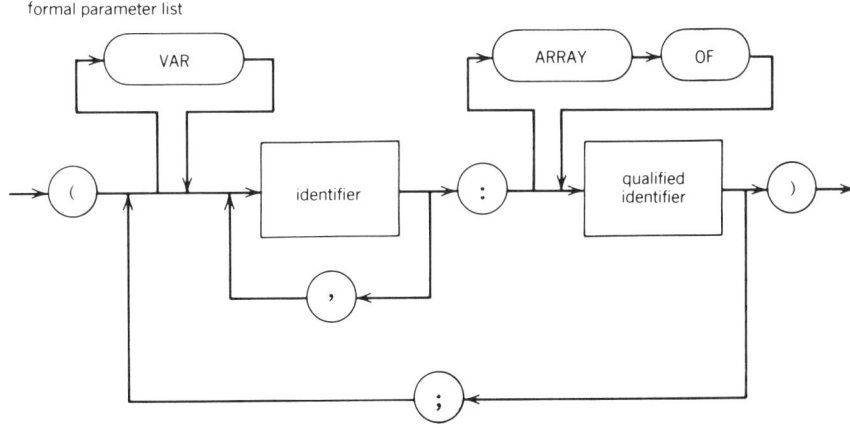

module declaration

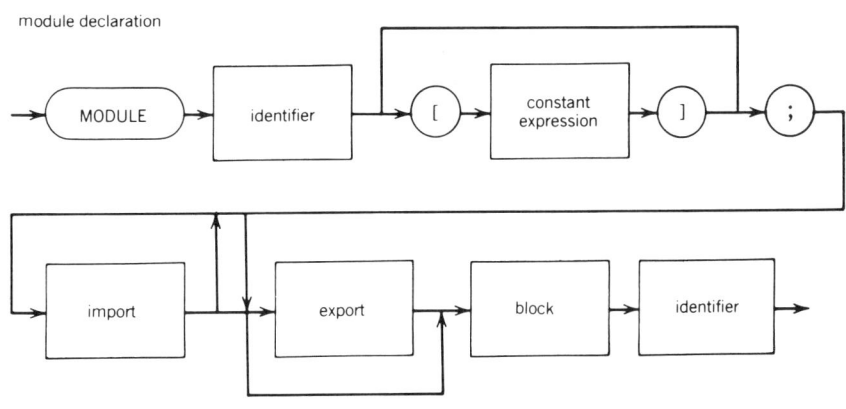

statement

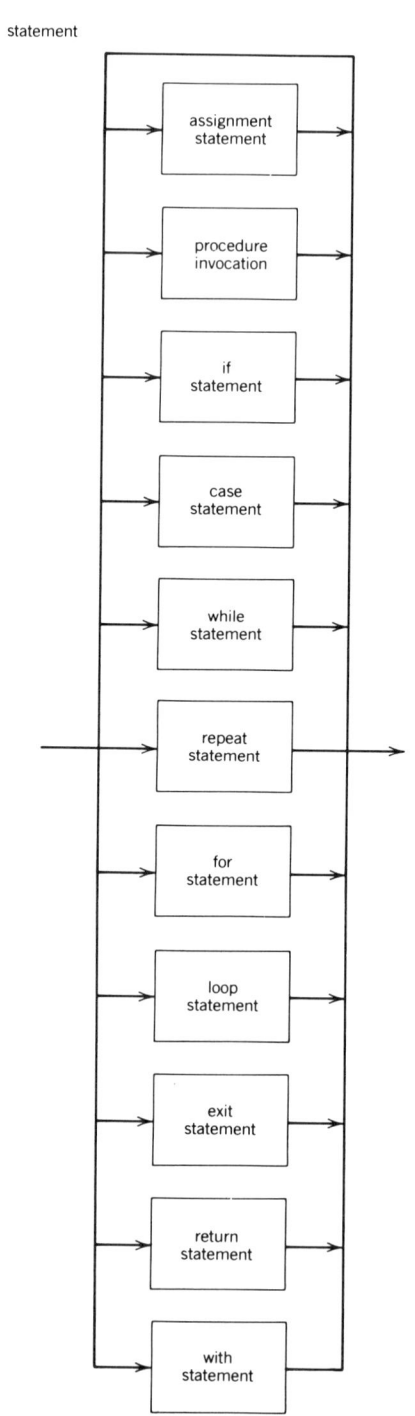

assignment statement

if statement

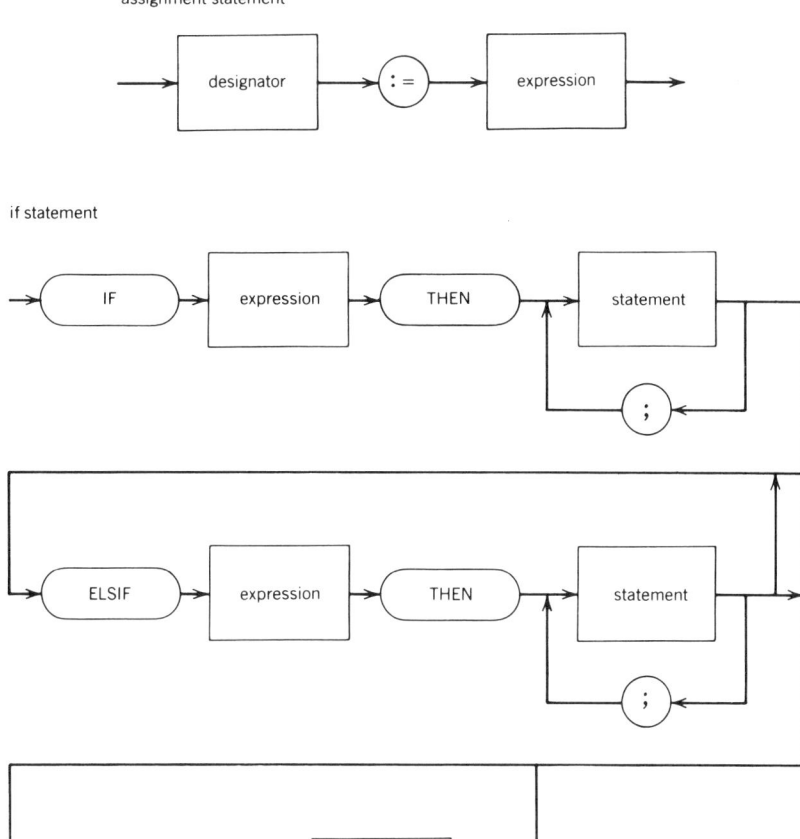

case statement

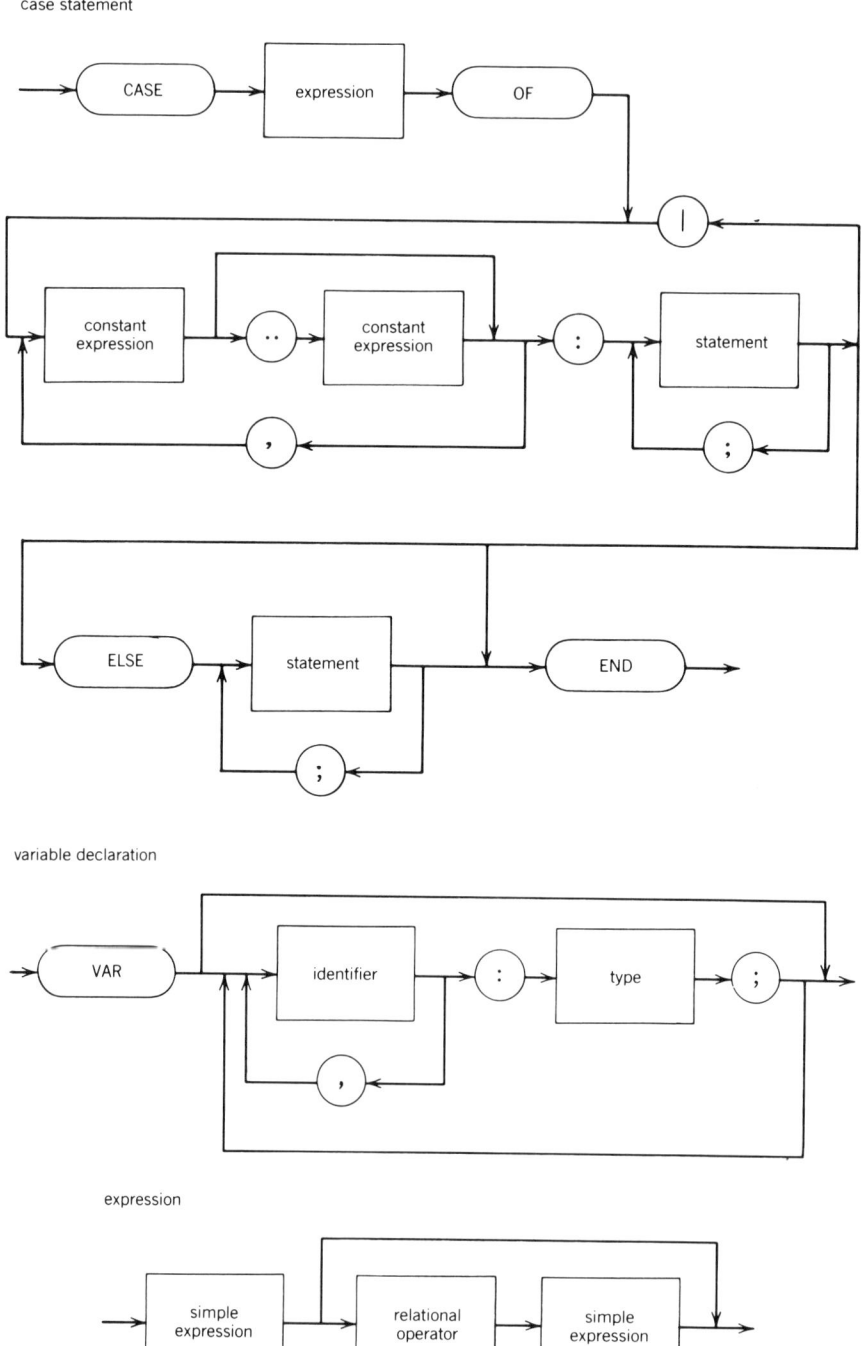

variable declaration

expression

simple expression

term

factor

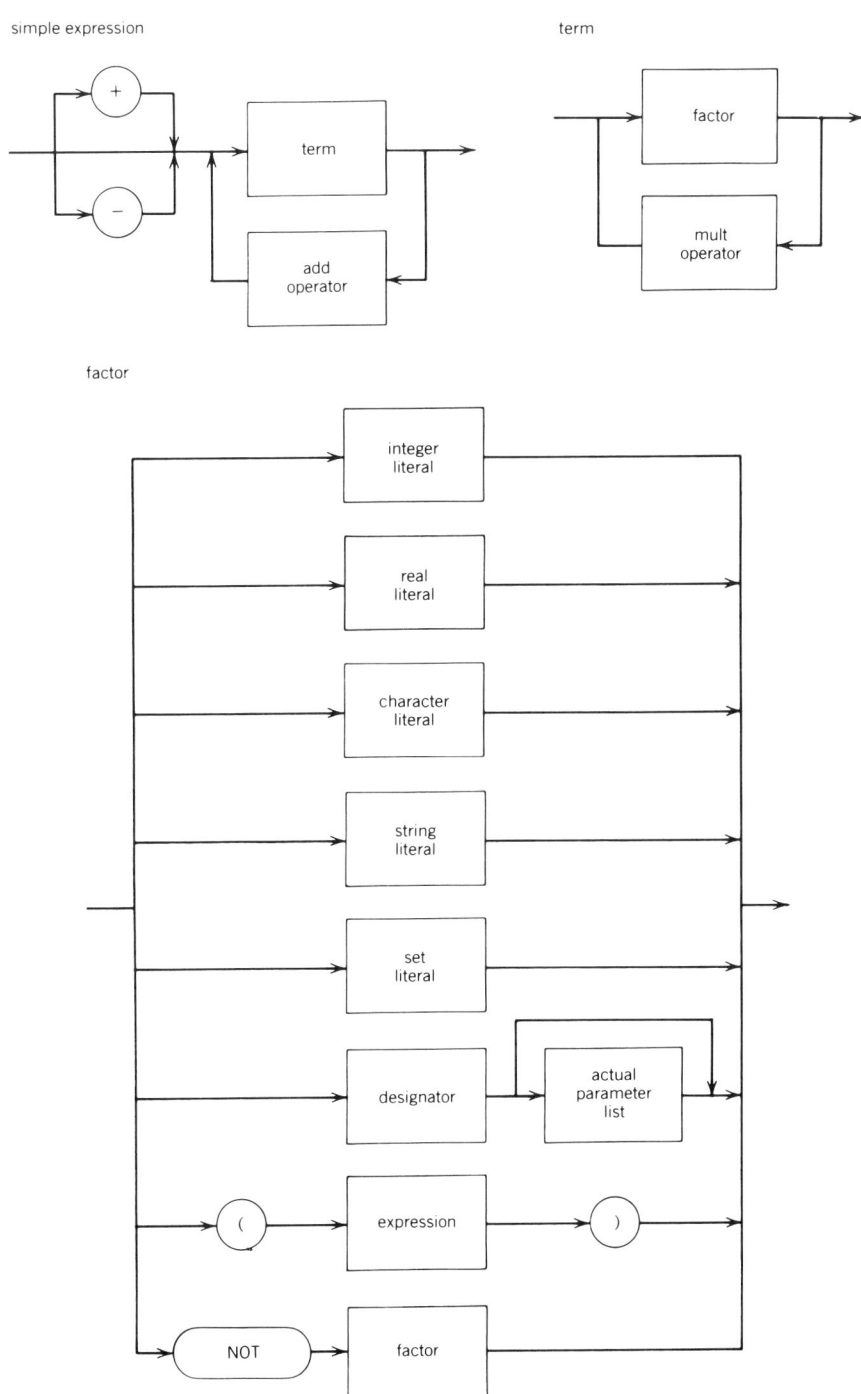

designator

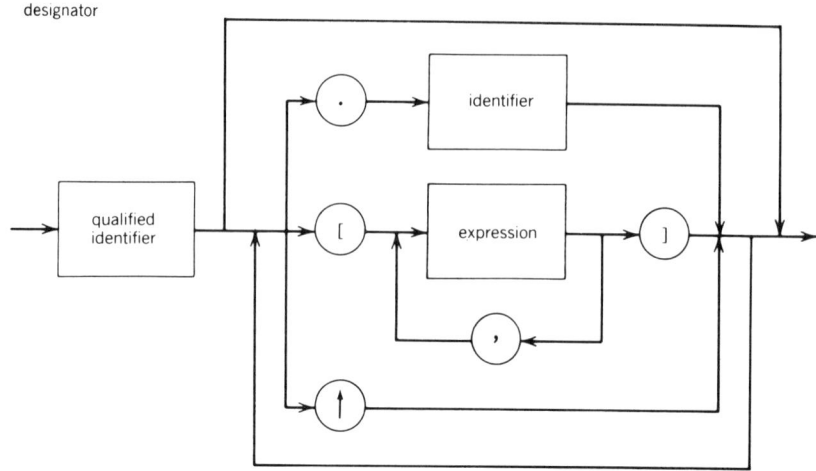

constant expression

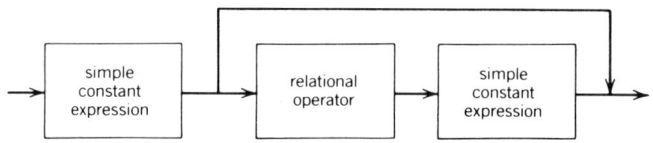

simple constant expression

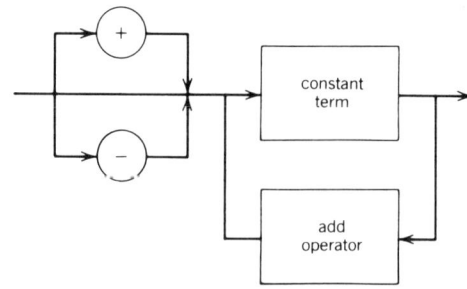

constant term

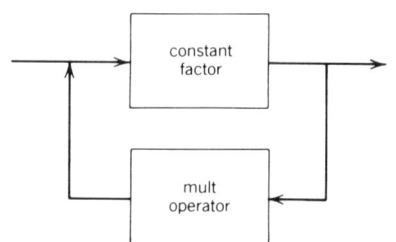

constant factor

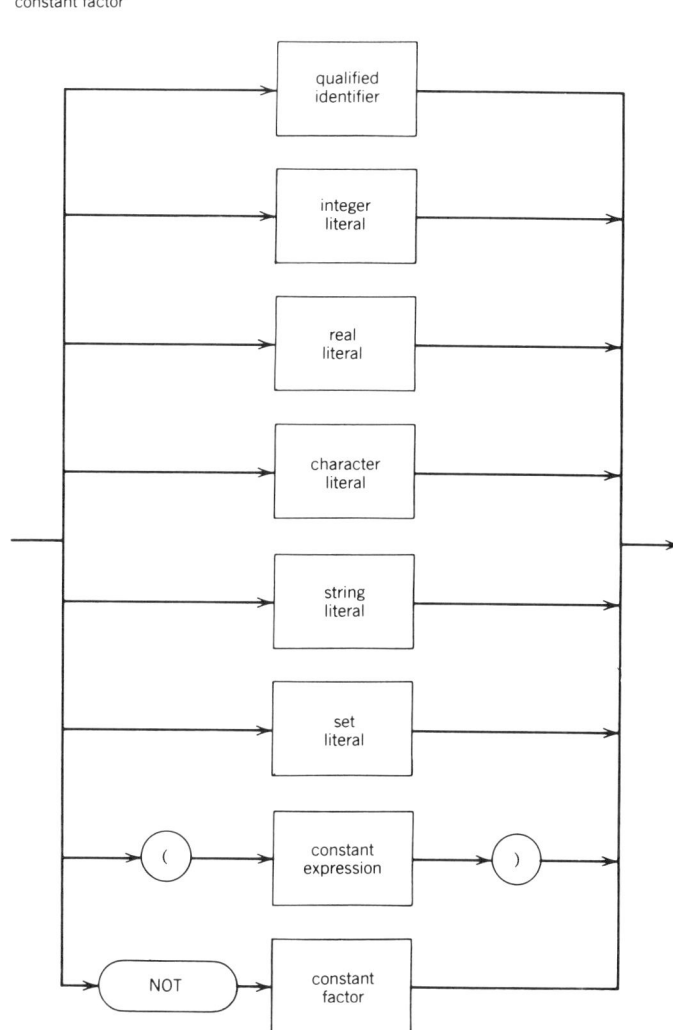

relational operator

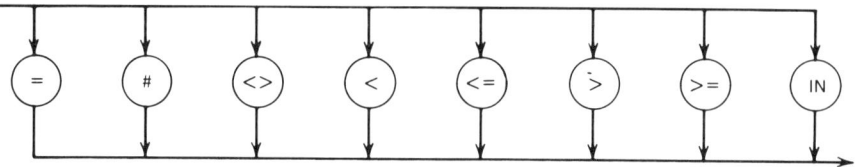

add operator

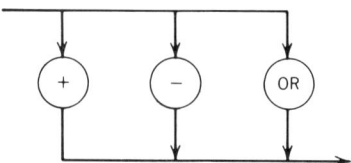

mult operator

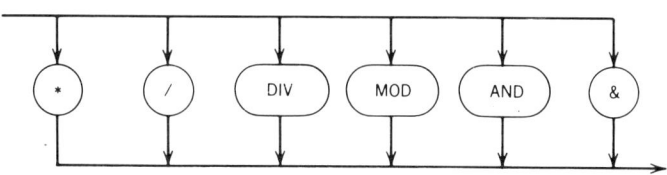

integer literal

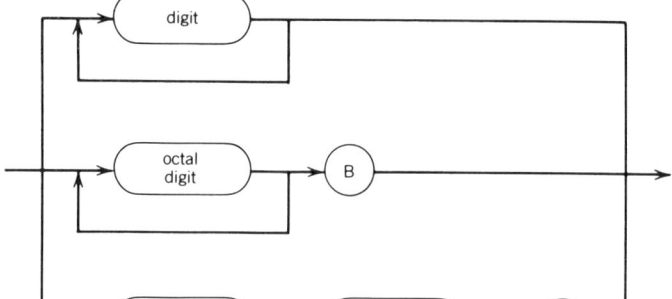

real literal

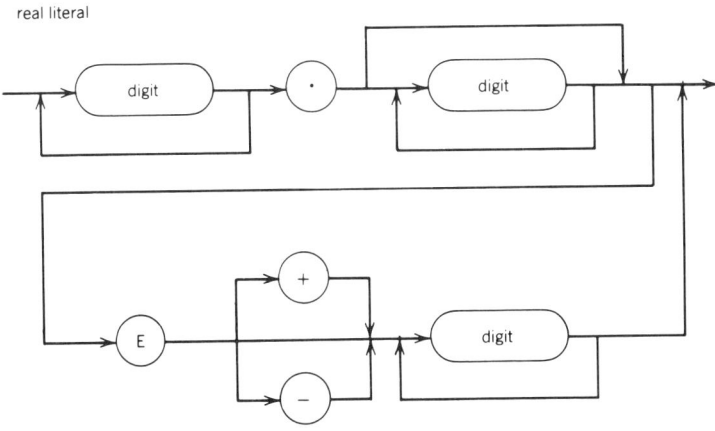

character literal

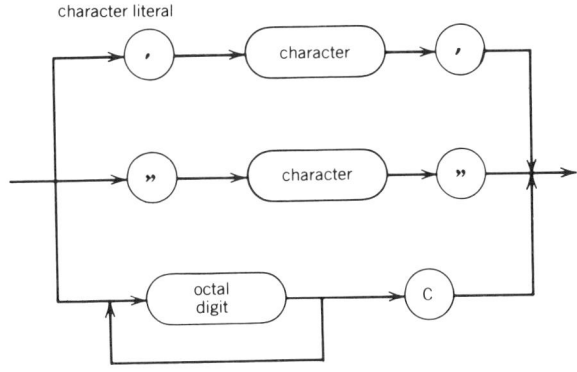

string literal

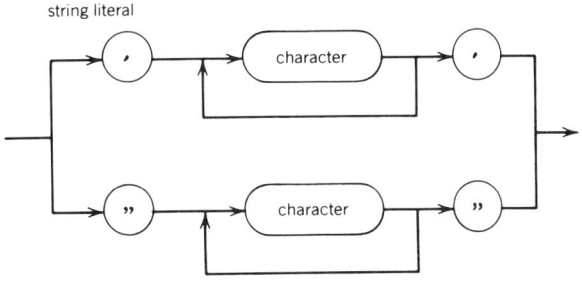

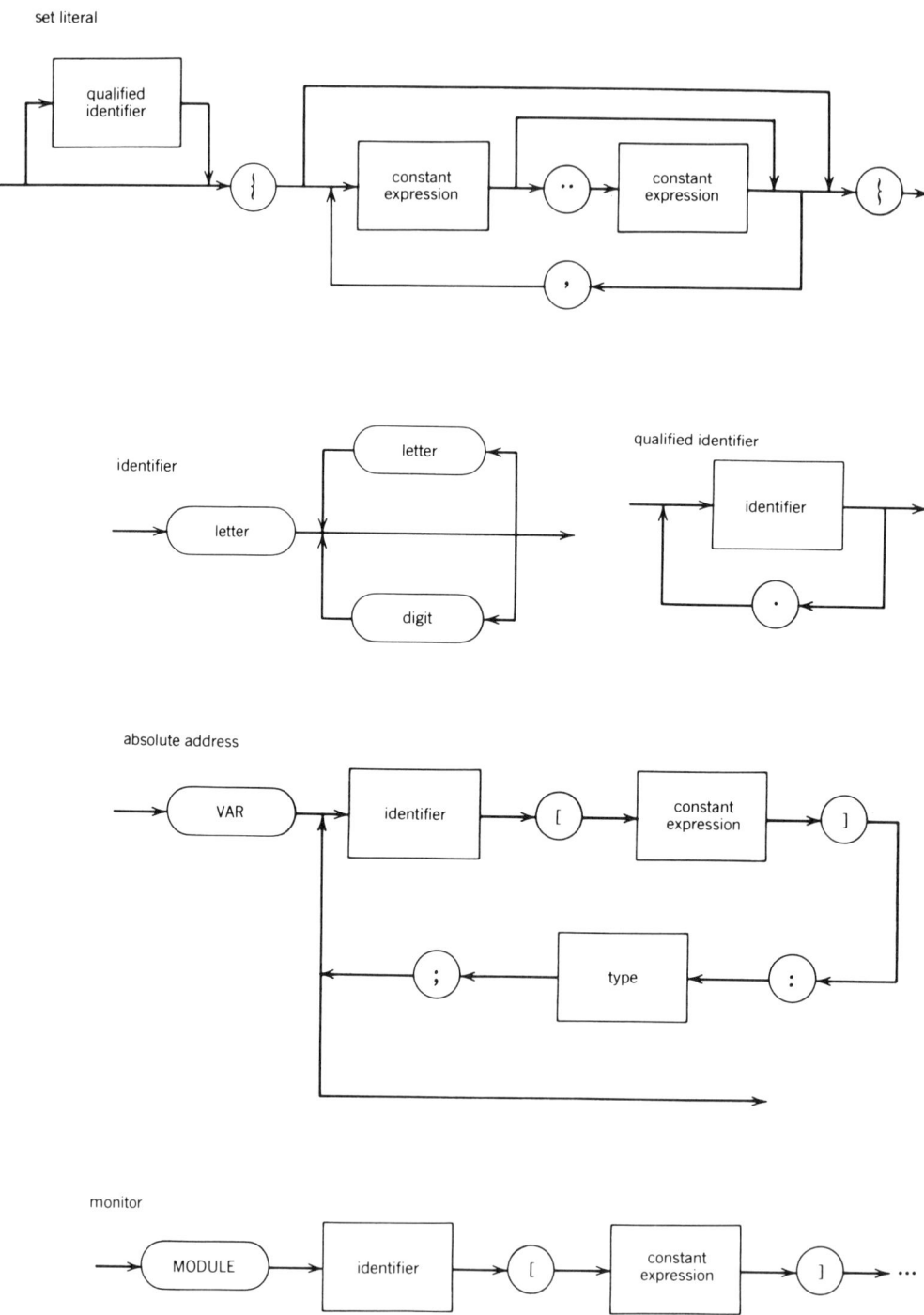

set literal

identifier

qualified identifier

absolute address

monitor

while statement

repeat statement

for statement

loop statement

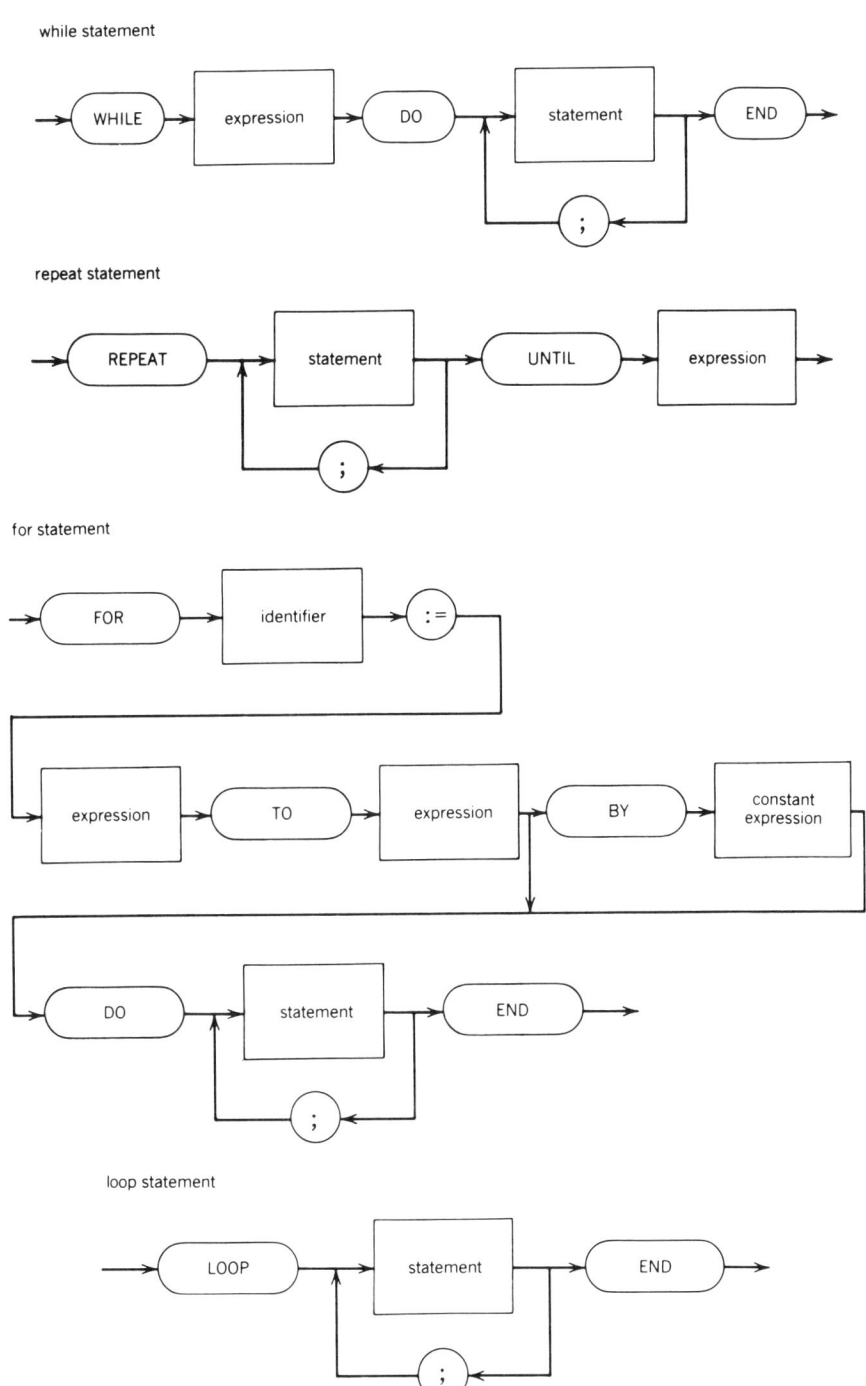

exit statement

with statement

procedure invocation

actual parameter list

return statement

constant declaration

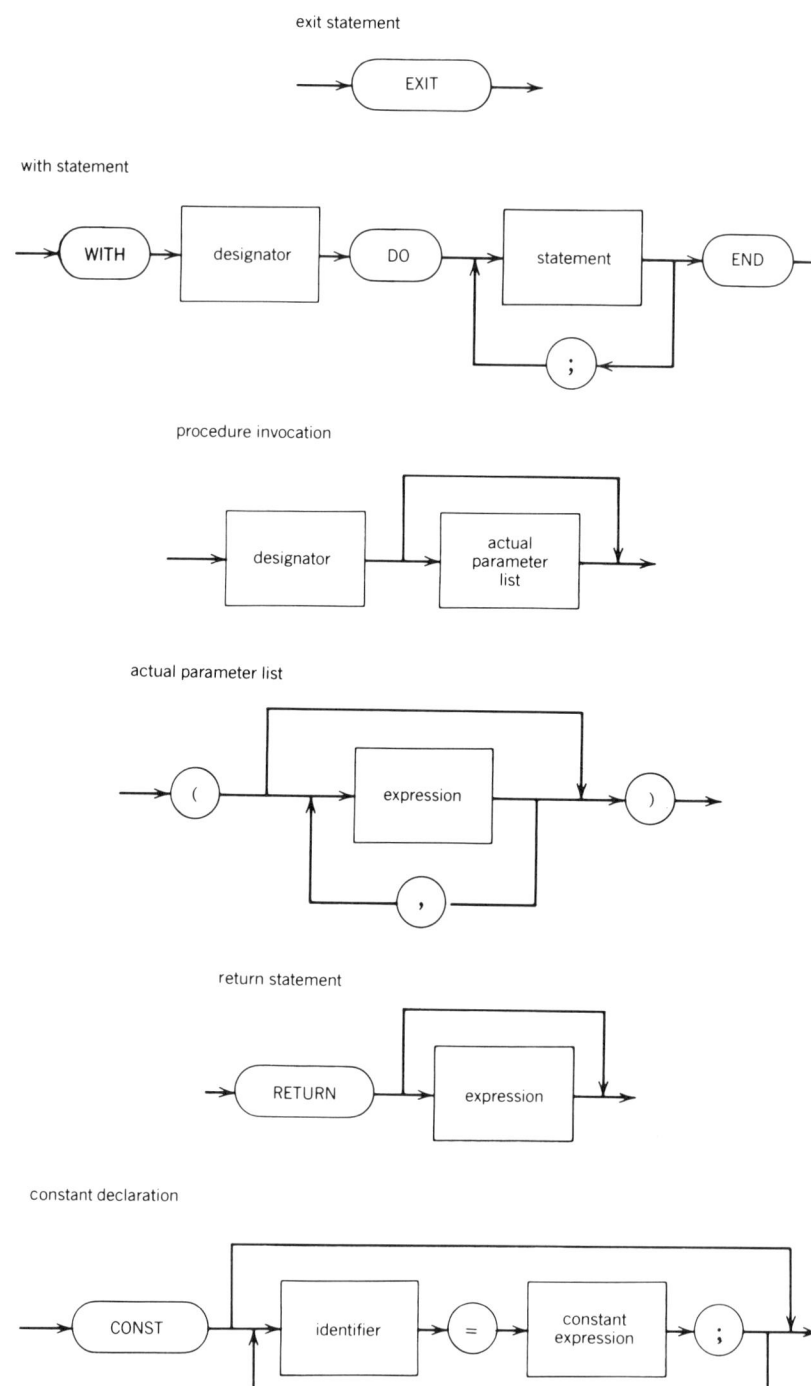

type declaration

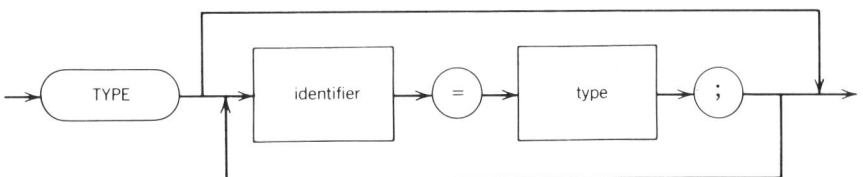

type

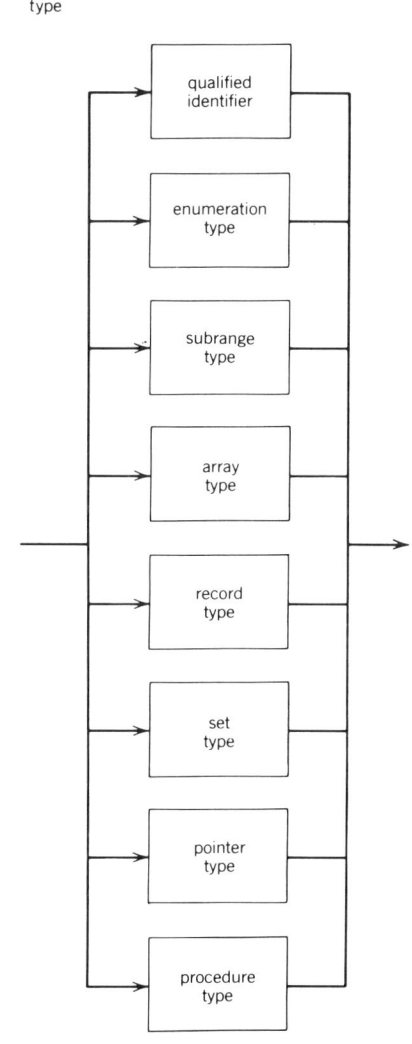

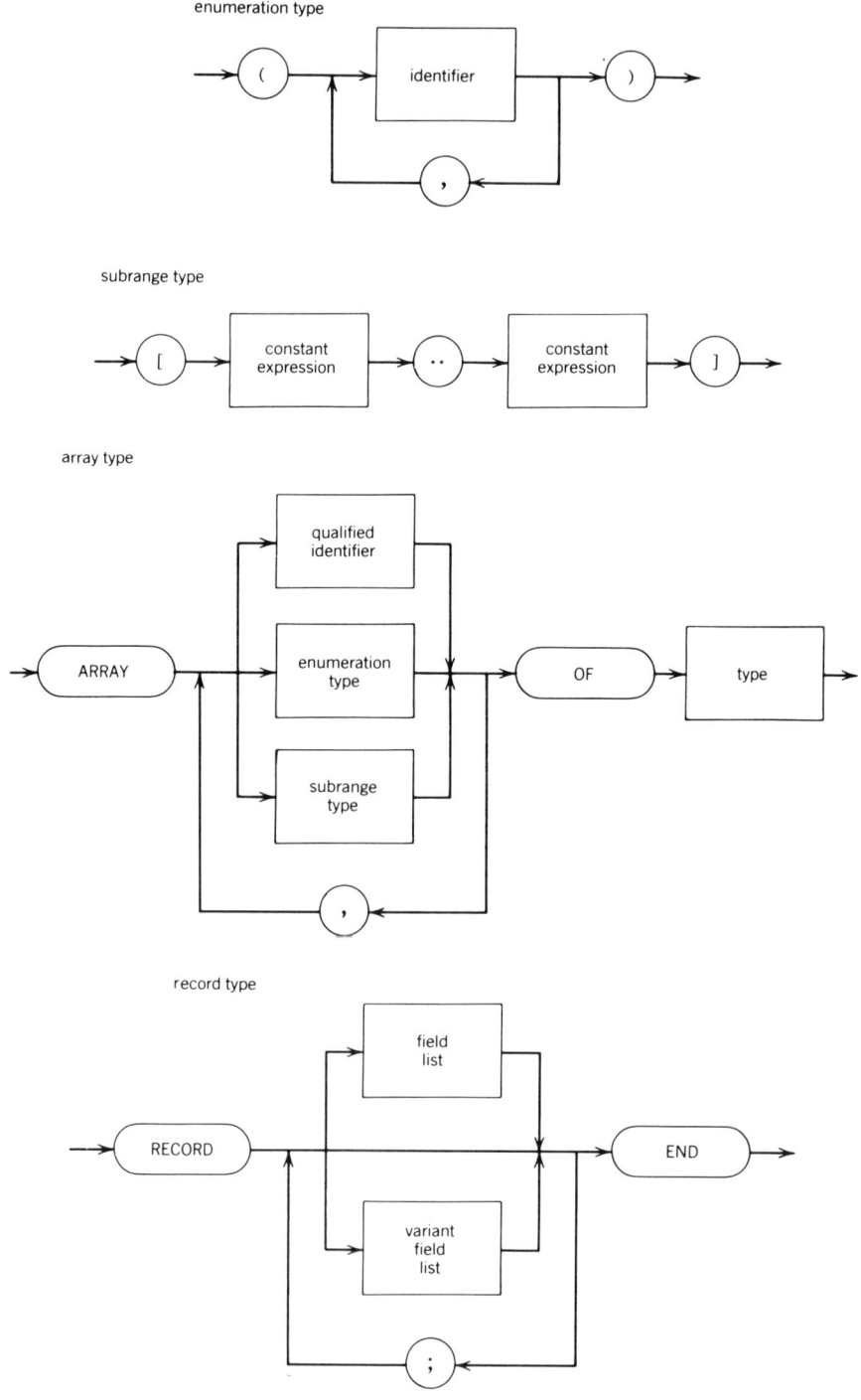

enumeration type

subrange type

array type

record type

field list

variant field list

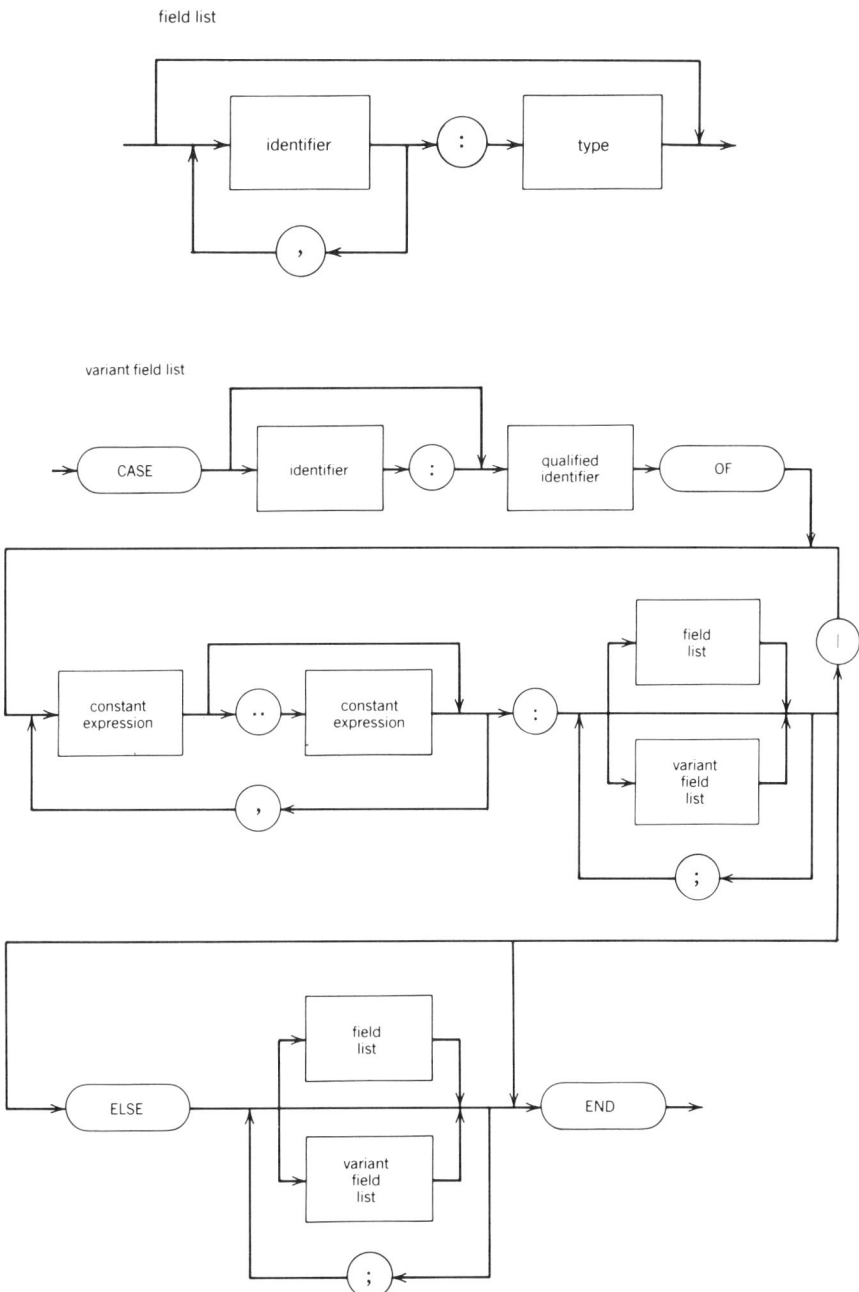

set type

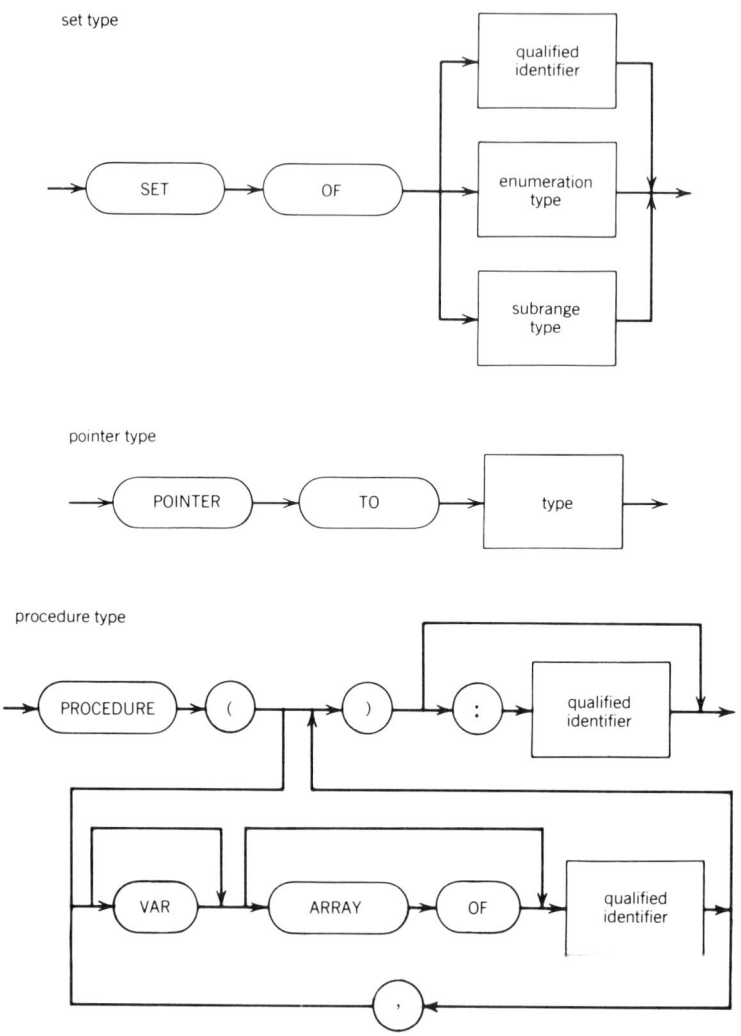

pointer type

procedure type

# Modula-2 Reserved Words, Operators, Delimitors, and Predefined Procedures

## Modula-2 Reserved Words

| | |
|---|---|
| AND | LOOP |
| ARRAY | MOD |
| BEGIN | MODULE |
| BY | NOT |
| CASE | OF |
| CONST | OR |
| DEFINITION | POINTER |
| DIV | PROCEDURE |
| DO | QUALIFIED |
| ELSE | RECORD |
| ELSIF | REPEAT |
| END | RETURN |
| EXIT | SET |
| EXPORT | THEN |
| FOR | TO |
| FROM | TYPE |
| IF | UNTIL |
| IMPLEMENTATION | VAR |
| IMPORT | WHILE |
| IN | WITH |

## Modula-2 Operators and Delimiters

| | |
|---|---|
| + | unary plus, addition, set union |
| – | unary minus, subtraction, set difference |
| * | multiplication, set intersection |
| / | real division, symmetric set difference |
| := | assignment |
| & | Boolean and |
| = | equal |
| < > | not equal |
| # | not equal |
| > | greater than |
| < | less than |
| ≥ | greater than or equal, superset |
| ≤ | less than or equal, subset |
| ^ | pointer dereference |
| ( ) | parentheses |
| [ ] | array index brackets, subrange brackets |
| { } | set braces |
| (* *) | comment delimiters |
| .. | subrange delimiter |
| . | period, qualified identifier |
| , | used to separate entities |
| ; | used as separator between lines of code |
| \| | used in case statements |

## Modula-2 Predefined Functions and Procedures

| | |
|---|---|
| ABS | (Absolute value) Operates on all numeric types. |
| INC | Increment, operates on integer and cardinal types. |
| DEC | Decrement, operates on integer and cardinal types. |
| ODD | Odd, operates on the cardinal type. |
| CAP | Uppercase, operates on the character type. |
| ORD | Ordinal, operates on character types and other enumeration types. |
| VAL | Value, operates on character types and other enumeration types. |
| TRUNC | Truncation, operates on the real type. |
| FLOAT | (Conversion to floating point) Operates on integer and cardinal types. |
| INCL | Include, operates on the set type. |
| EXCL | Exclude, operates on the set type. |

# ASCII Character Set

## ASCII Character Set

| First Digits | Last Digits | | | | | | | |
|------|------|------|------|------|------|------|------|------|
|      | 0    | 1    | 2    | 3    | 4    | 5    | 6    | 7    |
| 00   | nul  | soh  | stx  | etx  | eot  | enq  | ack  | bel  |
| 01   | bs   | tab  | lf   | vt   | ff   | cr   | so   | si   |
| 02   | dle  | dc1  | dc2  | dc3  | dc4  | nak  | syn  | etb  |
| 03   | can  | em   | sub  | esc  | fs   | gs   | rs   | us   |
| 04   | sp   | !    | "    | #    | $    | %    | &    | ,    |
| 05   | (    | )    | *    | +    | ,    | −    | .    | /    |
| 06   | 0    | 1    | 2    | 3    | 4    | 5    | 6    | 7    |
| 07   | 8    | 9    | :    | ;    | <    | =    | >    | ?    |
| 10   | @    | A    | B    | C    | D    | E    | F    | G    |
| 11   | H    | I    | J    | K    | L    | M    | N    | O    |
| 12   | P    | Q    | R    | S    | T    | U    | V    | W    |
| 13   | X    | Y    | Z    | [    | \    | ]    | ^    | --   |
| 14   |      | a    | b    | c    | d    | e    | f    | g    |
| 15   | h    | i    | j    | k    | l    | m    | n    | o    |
| 16   | p    | q    | r    | s    | t    | u    | v    | w    |
| 17   | x    | y    | z    | {    | \|   | }    |      | del  |

# APPENDIX
# 4

# References and Resources

## Books

Ford, Gary A., and Wiener, Richard S. *Modula-2: A Software Development Approach*. New York: Wiley, 1986.

Gleaves, Richard. *Modula-2 for Pascal Programmers*. New York: Springer Verlag, 1984.

Greenfield, Stuart B. *Invitation to Modula-2*. Princeton: Petrocelli Books, 1985.

Pinson, Lewis J.; Sincovec, Richard F.; and Wiener, Richard S. *Introduction to Computer Science Using Modula-2*. New York: Wiley, 1987.

Sincovec, Richard F., and Wiener, Richard S. *Data Structures Using Modula-2*. New York: Wiley, 1986.

Sincovec, Richard F., and Wiener, Richard S. *Modula-2 Software Components*. New York: Wiley Professional Software, 1987.

Walker, Billy K. *Modula-2 Programming with Data Structures*. Belmont: Wadsworth, 1986.

Wiener, Richard S., and Sincovec, Richard F. *Software Engineering with Modula-2 and ADA*. New York: Wiley, 1984.

## Periodicals

*ACM SIGPLAN NOTICES:* a monthly publication of the Special Interest Group on Programming Languages. Richard L. Wexelblat, Editor-in-Chief.

*Journal of Pascal, ADA, and Modula-2*: published six times per year by John Wiley and Sons, New York. Richard S. Wiener, Editor-in-Chief.

Appendix 4

# Index

Abstraction
   data, 94
   functional, 65
   process, 106-111
ABS function, 49
ADDRESS type, 99, 168, 169
ADR procedure, 99
Aliasing, 36
Alive variables, 92, 94
ALLOCATE, 35-36
AND, defined, 18
Apostrophes, literals and, 6
Arrays, 23-25
   assignment of, 46
   parameters and, 67
ASCII character set, 20
ASCII standard module, 158
Assignment statement, compatibility of, 44

Base set, 29
Base type, defined, 22
Binary standard module, 158
Binding modes, 65, 66
BITSET, 29
BITSET literals, 8
Bitstrings, 8
Bitvectors, 29
Bit manipulation, low-level, 100-104
Boolean data type, 18
Boolean literals, 6
Borland Turbo Modula-2, 168-176
Bottom-testing loop, 59
Branching structures, 51-56
Byte manipulation, 100-104
BYTE type, 98

CAP function, 49, 50
Cardinal data types, 15
CASE statement, 55, 168, 170
Changes in Modula-2, recent, 168

Character literals, 6
Character type (CHAR), 20, 168, 170
   strings and, 26
CHR function, 47
Comments, 9
Compilation, 83
   order of, 84
   Pascal and, 114
Compiler directive comments, 9
Constant declarations, 11
Constants, expression of, 12, 168, 169
Control characters, 7
Control structures, sequence, 51
Convert standard module, 159
ConvertReal standard module, 160
Coroutines, 106-111
   Pascal and, 114
CP/M Modula-2, 168

Dangling pointer, 38
Data abstraction, 94
Data hiding, 89, 94
   Pascal and, 114
Data structures, dynamic, 40-42
Data types, 15-34. See also name of specific
   data type
DEALLOCATE, 35-36
Declarations
   cardinal, 16
   constant, 11
   type, 13
   variable, 14
DEC function, 49, 50
Define procedure, 102-104
Definition modules, 82-88. See also name of
   module
   defined, 86
   for module termio, 133-139
   Turbo Modula-2 and, 170
Delimiters, 10

UCSD Pascal, 114
Uninitialized pointers, 39
Union operation, 31
UNIT, 114
UNTIL statement, 59

Value parameters, 66, 67
VAL function, 47, 49
VAR, 67, 170
Variables
  assignment of, 46
  global, 71-72, 92

  initialization code and, 81
  local, 71-72
  pointer. <u>See</u> Pointer variables
  static, 92
Variable declarations, 14
Variant records, 28, 168, 170
Version control systems, 85

WHILE loop, 57, 61
WORD type, 98
WRITELN, 171